THE
GRAND CANAL OF IRELAND

INLAND WATERWAYS HISTORIES

Edited by Charles Hadfield

The Ballinamore & Ballyconnell Canal. By Patrick Flanagan
The Bude Canal. By Helen Harris and Monica Ellis
The Dorset & Somerset Canal. By Kenneth R. Clew
The Grand Canal of Ireland. By Ruth Delany
The Grand Junction Canal. By Alan H. Faulkner
The Great Ouse. By Dorothy Summers
The Kennet & Avon Canal. By Kenneth R. Clew
The Leicester Line. By Philip A. Stevens
London's Lost Route to Basingstoke. By P. A. L. Vine
London's Lost Route to the Sea. By P. A. L. Vine
The Nutbrook Canal. By Peter Stevenson
The Royal Military Canal. By P. A. L. Vine
The Somersetshire Coal Canal and Railways. By Kenneth R. Clew
The Thames & Severn Canal. By Humphrey Household
The Yorkshire Ouse. By Baron F. Duckham

in preparation

The Birmingham Canal Navigations, Vol I. By S. R. Broadbridge
The Derby Canal. By Peter Stevenson
The Exeter Canal. By Kenneth R. Clew
The Forth & Clyde Canal. By Graham Matheson and D. Light
The Grand Western Canal. By Helen Harris
The Leicester Navigation. By Philip A. Stevens
The Oxford Canal. By Hugh Compton
The Shropshire Union Canals. By H. Robinson
The Stroudwater Navigation. By M. A. Handford
The Warwick Canals. By Alan H. Faulkner

THE GRAND CANAL
OF IRELAND

by

RUTH DELANY

With 33 plates and 24 text illustrations
including maps

DAVID & CHARLES: NEWTON ABBOT

ISBN 0 7153 5972 X

Set in 11pt Garamond, 2pt leaded
and printed in Great Britain
by Latimer Trend & Company Ltd Plymouth
for David & Charles (Holdings) Limited
South Devon House   Newton Abbot   Devon

TO
DOUGLAS

Contents

Contents

List of Illustrations

9

MAPS AND ILLUSTRATIONS IN TEXT

The maps are based on the Ordnance Survey by permission of the Government of the Republic of Ireland (Permit No 1768).

Preface

WHEN completing my late husband's book, *The Canals of the South of Ireland*, some years ago, I was fascinated by the wealth of detail in the minute books of the court of directors of the Grand Canal Company. I promised myself a closer study of them and in this book I have tried to tell the full story of the company as it was unfolded for me in the pages of the records. It is, therefore, the story of the company rather than the canal and includes its other activities such as the attempt to open up collieries in county Leix and its period of control of the middle Shannon from 1801 to 1840. It was difficult to decide how to present the material. I felt that a chronological approach, while it would have brought out the tremendous pressure of events at times on the directors, would have been confusing to the reader. In deciding to adopt a subject approach, I have had to move backwards and forwards in time which I hope will not prove equally confusing.

RUTH DELANY

CHAPTER 1

The Early Years

CANAL construction in Ireland in the early years, unlike elsewhere in the United Kingdom, was financed entirely from
government sources. The Act 2 Geo I, c 12 (Ir), 1715, authorised extensive navigation schemes and further acts in 1721 and
1729 appointed people to administer these works, at first on a
local and then on a provincial basis.[1] Some work was achieved;
the Newry Canal was constructed between 1731 and 1742 and
the Coalisland Canal was commenced in 1732.[2] It was not,
however, until 1751, when the commissioners were incorporated into a single body, the Corporation for Promoting and
Carrying on an Inland Navigation in Ireland, that interest in
canal construction began in earnest.[3]

One of the schemes authorised by the Act of 1715 had been
a proposal to link Dublin with the rivers Shannon and Barrow
but, apart from a few preliminary surveys, no steps were taken
to implement the plans.[4] In 1755 the scheme was revived and
it is the story of the construction of this canal, the Grand
Canal, which we are about to consider.

The main line runs for 26 miles from Dublin to the summit
level near Robertstown, 279ft above sea level, passing through
eighteen locks (four of them double locks*). From the summit
at Lowtown, the Barrow Line turns south through Rathangan
and Monasterevan to join the River Barrow at Athy, a distance of 28½ miles with nine falling locks (two double). The
Shannon Line runs west from Lowtown through Daingean

* A staircase pair in Ireland is called a double lock and is counted as one lock.

(Philipstown) and Tullamore to join the River Shannon near Banagher, a distance of 53 miles with eighteen falling locks (one double). With branches to Ringsend (forming the link with the River Liffey), Corbally, Mountmellick, Edenderry, Kilbeggan and Ballinasloe, the total mileage of the system exceeded 160 miles. Although there are three fine aqueducts and a number of smaller ones, there are no inclined planes, lifts or tunnels, but the canal does present a remarkable engineering achievement, because for many miles it was constructed through difficult bog terrain.

In 1755 and 1756 a considerable public controversy arose concerning the most advantageous route for the canal from Dublin to the Shannon.[5] Eventually it was agreed that a more southerly line, which had become known as the 'Grand' route, should be adopted, but it is interesting to note that the plans for a more northerly (or 'Royal') route were subsequently unearthed and used by the rival Royal Canal Company. Thomas Omer, who had been responsible for the surveys of the 'Grand' route, was appointed engineer in charge of the scheme by the Commissioners of Inland Navigation and work commenced in 1756.

In the years that followed Omer submitted progress reports to the Irish Parliament and further grants were authorised.[6] In 1763 he reported that, commencing at Clondalkin (5 miles outside the city), he had completed a canal for 12 miles to the west with three locks, six bridges (some of them wooden), seven aqueducts and four lock-houses. £57,000 (Ir)* had been spent, but he explained that he did not have sufficient funds to purchase the land required to bring the canal into the city.

In that year, 1763, Dublin Corporation began to take an interest in the canal as a possible source of water to supplement the Dodder supply to the city basin, and the commissioners authorised it to take over the construction of the canal.[7] Omer,

* Irish currency, £13 (Ir) equalled £12 (Br), was used until January 1826. See *Author's Notes.*

increasingly in demand at other navigation schemes, ceased to play an active part in the work, and the corporation proceeded, assisted by further parliamentary grants. In 1766 the contractors reported that the canal was ready to receive the water from the River Morrell, although it is clear from subsequent events that the city end of the canal had not yet been completed. When the water was turned in the banks gave way in several places and a second attempt to fill the canal, when repairs had been carried out, met with the same result.[8] Two years later, frustrated by inefficient contractors, the corporation decided to appoint an engineer, John Trail, to supervise the work. In the following year, 1769, Trail presented an encouraging report to the Irish Parliament and it was revealed by the secretary to the commissioners that over £200,000 (Ir) had been spent since 1755 in efforts to connect the River Barrow, Shannon and Boyne.[9] This included money spent on improving the river navigations and it would appear from some figures produced later in the Grand Canal Company records that about £77,000 (Ir) had been spent by this time on the canal, including payments of over £10,000 (Ir) to Dublin Corporation.

In 1770 a group of noblemen and merchants decided to try to form a company to take over the undertaking. Their efforts were successful, the Irish Parliament willingly accepted their proposals and on 2 June 1772 the Company of the Undertakers of the Grand Canal was incorporated.[10] All the 'powers, privileges, advantages and authorities' of the Commissioners of Inland Navigation were transferred to the new company, which was authorised amongst other things to sell redundant water, to erect turnpikes on the trackways and to charge tolls for freight not exceeding 3d (Ir) per ton per mile* and fares of 2d (Ir) per mile for passengers. Dublin Corporation, although reluctant to surrender control of the canal, decided to co-operate with the new company and a subscription of £10,000 (Ir) was voted to ensure a voice in its management. It was agreed that

* Probably Irish miles (2,240yd). See *Author's Notes*.

the canal company would receive 10 per cent of the gross annual receipts from pipewater revenue when supplies were commenced.[11]

The first recorded meeting of the company took place in 105 Grafton Street on 18 July 1772. There were 5 members present and the business was confined to an assessment of the financial situation. The next meeting discussed the administration to be adopted and it was agreed that a secretary, pay clerk, storekeeper and engineer should be appointed. Richard Baggs was subsequently appointed to the joint position of secretary and pay clerk at an annual salary of £150 (Ir) and John Trail agreed to enter into a contract to complete the canal from the city basin to the River Liffey near Sallins; he was to receive 5 per cent of all the money expended in carrying out this work, £300 (Ir) per annum and the balance when he had completed his contract. It was decided that a court of 41 directors would be elected annually; a committee of 31 would superintend the construction work: 'In general said Committee are to manage and inspect every Matter and thing within their Department in such a Manner that the Business of the Company may be Carryed on with the greatest Prudence and Economy'. Two further committees were to superintend the accounts and stores. The attendance of the directors varied considerably in the early years. There was then no company chairman, the procedure being to elect a chairman at each meeting. A few names, however, begin to emerge as regular attenders, amongst them Sir Lucius O'Brien, MP, whose influence had helped to form the company,[12] Arthur Pomeroy, MP (afterwards Lord Harberton), Patrick Bean, an ironmonger, who supplied the company for many years, John Binns, a merchant, who subsequently broke away to form the rival Royal Canal Company, Redmond Morres, Robert Bonynge, Joseph Barrett, James Horan, Nicholas English, Abraham Wilkinson and Joseph Huband, a barrister, who was elected in 1777 and with the exception of a few years remained a director until his death in 1835.

It is difficult to ascertain how far the work had progressed

B

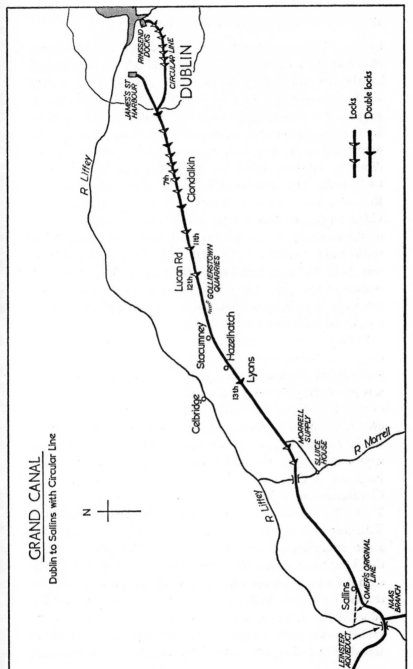

GRAND CANAL
Dublin to Sallins with Circular Line

N

R Liffey

RINGSEND DOCKS

CIRCULAR LINE

DUBLIN

JAMES'S ST HARBOUR

7th

Clondalkin

11th

Lucan Rd

12th

GOLLIERSTOWN QUARRIES

Stacumney

Hazelhatch

Celbridge

13th

Lyons

MORRELL SUPPLY

SLUICE HOUSE

R Morrell

R Liffey

Sallins

OMER'S ORIGINAL LINE

NAAS BRANCH

LEINSTER AQUEDUCT

Locks

Double locks

FIGURE I

by 1772. There is evidence that a second lock was under construction at Clondalkin and that the land had been purchased
for the city end of the canal but there was still a fall of over
100ft to overcome to reach the level of the city basin. In March
1773 the directors asked the Lord Lieutenant, Earl Harcourt, to
lay the foundation stone of the first lock. The ceremony was
performed on 15 April; thirty white rods were provided for the
directors, an army band was present and 'a few pieces of
Ordnance'. The assembled company then retired to the
Rotunda, where at 4 o'clock Mr Candy, of Church Street, provided 'an elegant dinner of two courses and a dessert' at a cost
to the company of 10s 6d (Ir) each 'excepting wine, syder,
spirits and spa water'. 'A plan of the intended lock of which the
first stone had been laid was raised in paste and adorned the
middle of the table. The whole was conducted in a manner
that gave honour to the judicious contriver, and the evening
concluded with harmonious festivity.'[13]

In the course of the summer the purchase of land continued;
the jury awarded an average of £6 (Ir) per acre (Ir) or 23 years
purchase to the landowners. John Trail reported that work
was proceeding building locks and sinking and banking parts
of the canal. The question of the future line of the canal, however, was uncertain, and opinions varied about the choice of
site for the crossing of the Liffey near Sallins. Two reports had
appeared in 1771, the first prepared by Charles Vallancey,
Engineer in Ordinary in Ireland since 1762, acting for the
Commissioners of Inland Navigation, and a second by John
Trail, who was at that time employed by Dublin Corporation.[14]
Vallancey criticised the selected crossing point and suggested
a site upstream, where there was a ford, but Trail explained
that Omer had in fact discarded this site and moved downstream to preserve the straight line of the canal. It will be
shown later that Vallancey's site was the one eventually
adopted but some of the excavations of the other line are
visible today which suggest that Omer intended to avoid an
aqueduct by locking down into the river and up again, although

Trail said that an aqueduct would be necessary because the other scheme would create problems in water supplies.

In the course of his report Trail had suggested that expert opinion should be sought on the controversial river crossing and other unsettled questions. Redmond Morres, one of the group trying to form the new company, asked John Smeaton, at that time engaged on the Forth & Clyde Canal, to come over to advise them.[15] At first reluctant, Smeaton eventually agreed to come in the summer of 1773, and bring an assistant who could stay to complete the survey. This assistant was to be William Jessop, later to become a well-known canal engineer in England and to act as consultant engineer to the Grand Canal Company until 1802.[16]

Morres, in the course of the correspondence, had asked Smeaton for advice on the administrative and practical side of canal building but the latter had replied that this was the most difficult of all subjects on which to comment. He recommended that the work should be done by contract and this was the system adopted by the company. J. Phillips, in his *General History of Inland Navigation*, published in 1792, quoted an example of a Grand Canal Company contract: Matthew Gamble undertook to sink the canal at prices varying from 3d (Ir) to 1s 10d (Ir) per cubic yard according to the difficulty of the terrain, 'the said Gamble finding his own powder, pumping water, and keeping tools, barrows and pumps in repair at his own expence till worn out, then the same to be returned to the Company's stores and replaced to the said Gamble by new ones . . . the said Gamble to draw subsistence weekly for the stone-cutters and labourers in proportion to their wages, and to have a general settlement once every quarter of a year'. Gamble had to produce 'two undeniable persons' each in £500 (Ir) security for the due performance of his contract.

Smeaton arrived in September 1773 and spent 14 days inspecting the line of the canal with Trail and Jessop. He submitted a short report before leaving Dublin and a second, which dealt in detail with the construction of canal through bog, in April 1775.[17] In his first report he criticised the line chosen through the Gollierstown quarries, 'but as the difficulty is in great part overcome, it does not seem now proper to depart from it'. He recommended a reduction in the overall proportions of the canal. Omer had envisaged a canal accommodating vessels of 170 tons and, as already mentioned, he had built three locks. These were 137ft long by 20ft wide and were at Clondalkin (11th lock), Lucan Road Bridge (12th lock) and Clonaughles or Lyons (13th lock). Trail had already decided to reduce the dimensions to 8oft by 16ft and the 1st lock (a double) and 2nd lock were built to these measurements at a total cost of £5,000. Smeaton suggested 60ft by 14ft with the channel of the canal 4ft 9in deep and 24ft wide at the bottom with slopes of 3ft to 4ft, which would accommodate vessels carrying about 40 tons, a more suitable size for the Irish trade because there would be less delay in obtaining full loads. Smeaton's measurements were adopted and Trail reduced the cost of the locks to about £1,000 each but, as it will be seen, some of them had to be rebuilt. Omer's locks were reduced to conform with the rest of the line by shortening them and narrowing the entrances and exits, giving them an unusual shape. The original lower gate recesses are visible today below the 11th and 12th locks and at 13th lock the stone facing was used for the lower gates when it was converted into a double lock in 1783. In that year a lock at Stacumney, which Trail had constructed to overcome an error in Omer's levels, was abandoned and the 13th lock converted into a double. Three of Omer's lock-houses survive, similar in design to those he constructed on the Shannon navigation at about the same time. Two of them, at 11th lock and Stacumney, where there was formerly a storeyard, are in ruins; but the third at 12th lock is still inhabited. The company subsequently built a lock-house here and Omer's house was used by the collector.

To return to Smeaton's report; he suggested that further investigation would be required to determine the site of the Liffey aqueduct. He was very critical of Omer's route through

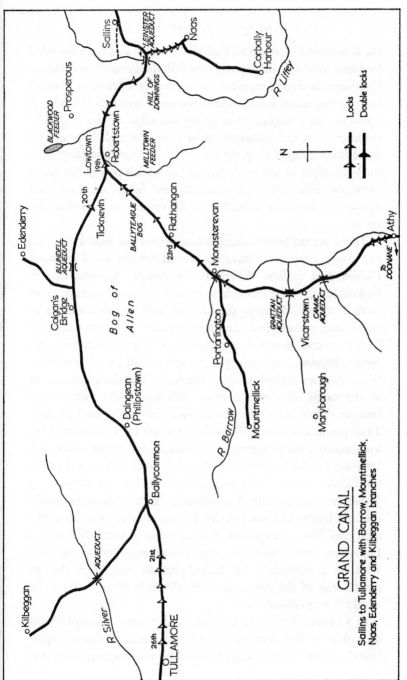

FIGURE 2

GRAND CANAL

Sallins to Tullamore with Barrow, Mountmellick,
Naas, Edenderry and Kilbeggan branches

the bog from Lowtown to Tullamore, which had been intended to carry out the dual purpose of drainage and navigation. Pointing out that there were much cheaper ways of reclaiming bog, he suggested a deviation to the north towards Edenderry, operating at a higher level along the edge of the bog. His comments on the construction of canal through bog will be more interesting if they are considered in the next chapter in the light of the actual work carried out on this part of the canal. Most of Smeaton's recommendations were adopted and Jessop remained in Ireland until November to complete the survey.

There are no board minutes entered for the next two years but work appears to have continued on the canal between Dublin and Sallins. When Trail's reports recommence in November 1775, he was able to inform the board that the gates were hung on all except the Morrell lock and that work was continuing sinking and banking the canal. The directors must have been confident that this part of the line was nearing completion because, early in 1776, they advertised for proposals for 'Executing an Aqueduct' over the Liffey and the continuation of the canal west of the river with two locks and several bridges. They were, however, over-optimistic, and in May Trail sounded the first discordant note.[18] He commenced his long report with the warning: 'I flattered Myself that this month I should be able to present a Report to you that would prove satisfactory to the real Friends of the Canal and pleasing to Myself but am severely disappointed.' He went on to complain that Mr Baggs had not provided the money to pay the workmen and 'this unexpected Stoppage has thrown Me into a Labyrinth from which My Extrication may yet be attended with some difficulty'. He added that he had been able to meet some of the payments with the help of friends but he would have to dismiss 200 men.

In October he wrote to Redmond Morres to explain his difficulties at Ballyfermot lock. He had not been able to supervise the work 'for my being confin'd by a very severe and painful disorder'. He had issued instructions but some members of the company had come along and ordered that the whole side of the lock would have to be taken down and rebuilt. He protested that in the twenty years of his professional career he had never experienced a similar failure. He went on to explain that he could not possibly rebuild the lock and complete his contract by the following February because he could not admit the water until the lock had dried out. He undertook to maintain the works for two years from the completion of his contract and to superintend the Liffey acqueduct for a salary of £300 (Ir) per annum, but the directors ignored this proposal and replied that he would have to use his own judgement about the lock.

Early in December the directors were infuriated by an announcement from Trail that he intended to hold an auction of stores at the Grand Canal storeyard. The stores were all listed and concluded with an NB: 'There are several Casks of clear Terras to be sold. . . . It is unnecessary to mention the great Utility of Terras Mortar in such pieces of Masonry as are intended to withstand water.' The directors promptly published a notice cancelling the sale, pointing out that Trail had not yet completed his contract. Trail attended the board, but his answers were not satisfactory and Mr Adam Williams was asked to prepare 'a General State of the Case' to lay before the Attorney-General.

On 14 January 1777 Trail resigned:

Gentlemen,
    Pursuant to Articles entered into between You and Me, I will on Tuesday the 21st Instant January at Eleven o'clock in the forenoon, attend on the Grand Canal at Sallins Bridge near the River Liffey in the County of Kildare, and from thence proceed to, and put you or such person or persons as you shall Authorize to receiveth the Same, into the possession of said Canal, Locks, Bridges, Houses, Storeyards, and all Appurtenances thereunto belonging, and from said Day I will Consider Myself free from any Charge or Risque attending said several Works, and My Contracts with you, on My part fully

and faithfully Compleated of which you as a Corporation, and every Person concerned are desired to take Notice.

I am Gentlemen Your very humble Servant,
John Trail

Ten post-chaises were ordered and, on the morning of 21 January, eight directors set off accompanied by Captain Tarrant, an engineer, who was to succeed Trail, Mr Adam Williams and seven other men 'of Knowledge in Masonry, Carpentry and Smithswork'. The meeting took place; the directors refused to accept that the canal from Sallins to the Morrell had been executed 'in the most perfect and Workman-like Manner as Mr Trail's Estimates and Contracts require'. The party then moved to the Morrell sluice house, Mr Trail handed over the key and the directors informed him that the canal from there to the city basin had not been completed to their satisfaction. Trail would not hand over the plans of the canal or answer any further questions, declaring that he would not 'take any further Charge or Risque of the said Works'.

A committee was appointed to deal with the suits to be instituted against Trail. His suggestion that arbitrators should be appointed to avoid litigation was turned down and on 16 September Benjamin Matthews was paid £5 5s (Ir) for his arrest. This is the last reference to the matter in the records but Trail's reputation does not appear to have been permanently damaged and he was subsequently knighted for his work in connection with Dublin Corporation.[19]

In the meantime Captain Tarrant's reports confirmed the board's worst fears. In April he reported that the dam in the level* above the Morrell lock had given way and at the 6th lock 'the ashlaring on the North side of the Chamber to an extent of 30ft in length and from Top to bottom of the Central Part, sprung out like a long bow'. A week later he wrote:

On Wednesday the 9th April the Lock East of the Morrell Lock having been thrice filled—that Day the Ashlaring of the South Wall of the Chamber burst. . . . I found the North and

* In Ireland the term 'level' is used instead of 'pound'.

South Walls of the Chamber bulged and lower wing wall over-hanging—after the first filling the Water being discharged there was a bubbling of muddy water at the foot of the Walls and a Discharge of the same thro' joints a bad omen of its condition.

Tarrant had to cope with other problems, such as cattle grazing on the towpaths and the removal of trees for maypoles. He recommended that each of the lock-keepers should be given a 'half pike halbert' to help him to enforce the company regulations. The directors issued an advertisement offering rewards for prosecution to conviction of certain offences: £10 10s (Ir) for injuring the company's boats, £5 13s 9d (Ir) for injuring locks or trees or abusing the company's officers, £1 2s 9d (Ir) for persons found swimming or washing in the water and 11s (Ir) for swimming dogs in the canal. There were disputes about water rights; on one occasion Tim Daly, a miller, and several of his men broke down the sluices at the Morrell in 'a violent and forceable manner'.

The board kept a watchful eye on the works and the committee of works was instructed to carry out weekly inspections. Captain Tarrant was asked to submit detailed monthly accounts, for example the account (Irish currency) for August 1777 read as follows:

	£	s	d
To Labourers, Horses and Carrs etc.	76	5	2
To Shipwrights etc.	30	7	0
To Carpenters and Sawyers	14	2	2
To Masons	23	8	7
On account of Quarrying	20	1	3
Iron work for Boats, Locks etc.	11	7	6
Lock-keepers	35	9	8
Total	211	1	4

The mention of boats and lock-keepers shows that by this time the completed sections of the canal were being used to carry materials. This is confirmed by an amusing letter from Walter

Costelloe in August 1777 seeking the contract, at 9d (Ir) per cubic yard, for bringing earth from the quarry at 3rd lock to bank the canal near the city basin:

> The delays of filling and going through the Locks which it puzzles me to think of how I shall goe safe thro' the Job and to save myself in it, if it be my look to get it which I know there is Several men means to bid for said work and some I am sure are not able to carry it on, nor neither do they know how they shou'd. Likewise Gentlemen whoever gets this Work will expect when begun they will have no delays they will Expect to get two Bigg Boats along with two Liters to have the Track Line and two Poles to help on the Boats where the Horse cannot draw them likewise to have the Levels kept full and the Locks attended by the Lock-keeper to give no Delays likewise the Use of half a dozen Barrows if wanting and proper subsistance Every week.

The supply of water to the city basin was commenced in August 1777 and a reminder was sent to Dublin Corporation of the 1772 agreement. Work continued over the winter months repairing and raising the banks where necessary, quarrying stone at Gollierstown, building boats and and rebuilding the faulty 6th lock. Side shores were cut to enable the supply of water to be maintained. The committee was able to report by June of the following year: 'The whole Line from the Bason to Sallins Bridge seems to be in a prosperous way. We think Captain Tarrant has acted with Skill and Prudence and if the Company will furnish Him with Money, are of the Opinion there may be a Compleat Navigation to Sallins this Season.'

The canal was opened to traffic on 2 February 1779. It was decided to offer a low toll to the first seven boats to operate on the canal: 1d per ton per mile and ¼d per lock and thereafter the charge would be 2d per ton per mile and ½d per lock (Irish currency and miles). By this time the company had eight boats carrying materials but four of these were 'too bad to be kept loaded for one night'. Thomas Digby Brooke was the first trader on the canal and in November 1779 he wrote to the board appealing for a reduction in tolls. In four months he had managed to make only twenty-seven trips 'owing to the per-

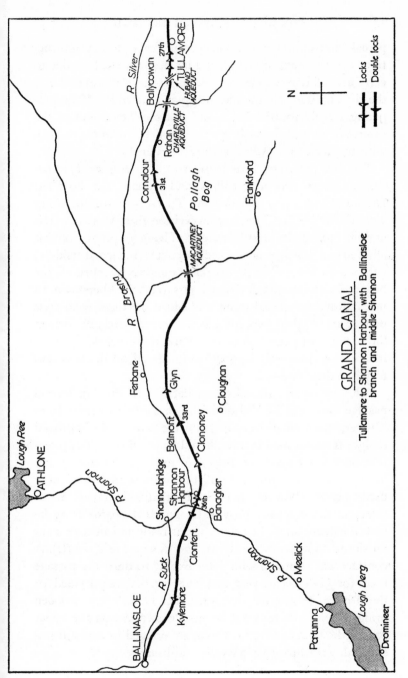

GRAND CANAL

Tullamore to Shannon Harbour with Ballinasloe
branch and middle Shannon

FIGURE 3

petual interruption of the Navigation from various obstructions and the want of water', and his boat was seldom able to carry her full burden. He was carrying stone, clay and coal into the city and dung on the return trip and, he added, 'I am preparing largely for the Brick and Potatoe Trade and in the Cource of another Season hope to open the Eyes of the Publick with respect to the Advantages of the Canal'.

The first passenger boat began to ply in August 1780 between Osberstown, near Sallins, and Dublin. The boat left Dublin at 6am every Monday and Thursday, returning every Tuesday and Friday. The covered division charge was 1s 1d (Ir) and the open division 6½d (Ir); 30lb of baggage per person was allowed and packages not exceeding 3cwt were carried at 6d (Ir) per cwt. In September the works committee travelled on the boat and reported that it took 9 hours to reach Osberstown, 18 miles away. A covered cabin was added for the second class passengers but they were forbidden to use the deck. No person 'in liquor' was permitted to travel and those behaving 'in an indecent or disorderly manner' were turned off the boat and forfeited their fare.

After two years the directors decided to build a second passage boat and Mr Edward Bird, a ship's carpenter from Chester, was invited over to build the boat to an improved design. It was agreed that he should be provided with protection on his passage from Bristol to prevent him from being 'impressed'. On 7 July 1783 all the boats on the canal were used to convey Volunteers to Sallins to attend a review at the Curragh; the company provided a hundred boards to make seats for them. Soon the new boat was ready and another commissioned to replace the original one, at a cost of £120 (Ir). A contract was arranged with John Buckly to draw the passage boats for £236 (Ir) per year, and four jackets were provided for the drivers. It was recommended that Omer's low wooden bridges should be replaced because 'passengers on the upper part of the boat to save their lives are obliged to throw themselves down whilst they pass the said bridges'.

Vallancey's site for the Liffey aqueduct had been adopted and work had begun in the spring of 1780. Richard Evans, an assistant engineer, had by this time taken over active control of the works with Tarrant submitting occasional reports. The latter had to relinquish one-quarter of his salary because of his absence and Evans received a gratuity of £70 (Ir) 'as a Proof of our Opinion of his Integrity and Attention to the Works of the Company'. Evans built two special boats to transport material on the River Liffey and when this work was completed, he erected platforms on them to form a temporary bridge.

While the aqueduct was being constructed, work proceeded on the line to Robertstown, and Thomas Black contracted to build the 17th and 18th locks. These were the last two rising locks leading to the summit level which was supplied by two feeders, the Milltown or 'Grand Supply' and the Blackwood supply. The Milltown feeder is nearly 8 miles long; it was extended in the 1790s, bringing in additional supplies, and commences at a pool fed by seven springs.[20] The Blackwood feeder was constructed as a reserve supply; it was 4 miles long with a reservoir at Foranfan.

It was increasingly difficult to find money to finance all this work. Petitions were made to the government from time to time but without success.[21] The forfeited shares of defaulters who had failed to complete their subscriptions were sold to try to raise funds. Trade on the canal was increasing rapidly and was further encouraged in 1783 when the charge for lockage was abandoned and tolls for freight were reduced to 1½d per ton per mile with a special rate of ½d per ton per mile (Irish currency) on lime, limestone, turf, building materials, gravel, soil and dung. It was found unsatisfactory to allow traders to have toll accounts and the lock-keepers were instructed to collect the tolls, receiving an increase of £2 2s (Ir) per annum for this extra duty, bringing their wages to £12 12s (Ir) per year.

There was a certain amount of rivalry between the boatmen.

The master of Darcey's boat, the *Good Intent*, was fined 'for acting unwarrantably' in cutting the trackline of Mr Alloway's boat, the *Duke of Leinster*, to prevent her from passing. The public was beginning to appreciate the advantages of water transport. The *Freeman's Journal* commented in August 1784:

> The collateral advantages of the navigation begin to operate already in various parts; particularly at Celbridge and its environs, which Mr Sisson has engaged to supply with coals to facilitate which, a subscription we hear is actually entering into by the gentlemen of that neighbourhood, for the purpose of a navigable cut from Celbridge to the Canal.

In October 1784 the passenger service was extended to Robertstown. The company decided to build a hotel at Sallins in that year and plans and an estimate of £1,500 (Ir), submitted by Mr Morrison, were accepted by the board. On 3 June 1788 the *Dublin Evening Post* reported that the Marquis and Marchioness of Buckingham had 'made a water excursion up the Grand Canal. . . . A coach accompanied the boat along the banks, which was to serve as a retreat in case the passage through the locks should prove disagreeable'. Two weeks later it reported:

> Water excursions up the Grand Canal, are now much in fashion, . . . nor can this seem extraordinary, when we reflect on the beauty of the country thro' which the canal passes, the excellent accommodations to be had in the passage boats, and the capital inn at Sallins, fitted up with peculiar neatness and admirably well kept.

An account of this hotel and the other hotels subsequently built by the company, together with a description of the growth of the passage-boat business, will be dealt with in Chapters 5 and 6.

CHAPTER 2

The Barrow and Shannon Lines

AT an early stage the court of directors had decided that it would be more practical to effect the junction with the Barrow before attempting the link with the Shannon, and work began on the Barrow Line in 1783. Thomas Black signed a new contract to construct two locks at Ballyteague bog for £750 (Ir) each with an undertaking to keep them in repair for seven years, and advertisements were issued seeking tenders for the earthworks of the canal to Monasterevan in lots of ½ mile (Ir). In September 1783 the *Freeman's Journal* reported:

> Last Tuesday the evaluation of the lands through which the Grand Canal is to be cut to Monasterevan was concluded to the satisfaction of all parties, the line being mostly through bog will, by drainage thereof, be of infinite service to the contiguous proprietors. The work of this great national undertaking is now carrying on with the greatest spirit at the bog of Ballyteague.

By May 1784 the committee of works reported 300 men working at Ballyteague and congratulated Evans on the anticipated completion of the canal to Monasterevan by the end of the year. Once again the directors were being over-optimistic. In November Evans reported that the terrain was proving more difficult than anticipated and he had to increase his estimates. In the spring of the following year Tarrant reappeared and, Evans complained, interfered with the works. The board assured him that he, Evans, was in charge but that in all matters of importance he should consult with 'our Superintendent' Tarrant. The latter discovered some discrepancies in the levels which necessitated the construction of an additional lock at Ballyteague and the conversion of Rathangan lock into a double.

Bernard and M. B. Mullins wrote a paper in 1846 entitled 'The Origin and Reclamation of Peat Bog with some Observations on the Construction of Roads, Railways and Canals in Bog', in which they referred to these mistakes.[1] It will be shown later that Bernard was engaged as an overseer when the canal was being constructed through the Edenderry bog and he subsequently started a partnership, Henry, Mullins & McMahon, who became the principal canal contractors in the country. Referring to the great difficulty experienced at Ballyteague, they said:

> the water was forced into the canal before a sufficient sectional area was obtained; and it was by dredging at a great expense and loss of time, that an imperfect navigable depth of canal was subsequently had; and so clumsy were the operations then carried on, . . . it was discovered, on the opening of the navigation, that a mistake of 4ft 6in had been made in the bog level.

This stretch of canal continued to cause trouble and in 1803–4 a new canal was cut through the bog, the additional lock (21st) was moved to the north end of the bog and the falls of the 20th and 21st locks equalised.

Volumes 5 and 6 of the company's records (August 1785 to August 1789) are missing, but it is possible to follow the progress of the work in the newspapers. On 15 January 1785 the *Dublin Evening Post* informed its readers that the canal would be completed to Monasterevan in less than a month. Finally on 20 October it was reported that a boat, the *Carlow Volunteer*, had entered the canal from the Barrow at Monasterevan, 'an event that must give pleasure to all who have this great inland navigation at heart'. The number of trade boats had increased to over eighty and boats came from as far away

Page 33 Early days: (*above*) 1st lock, Suir Road Bridge, built by Trail in 1773 to his larger measurements; (*below*) the silver trowel used by Earl Harcourt to lay the foundation stone and then presented to Trail

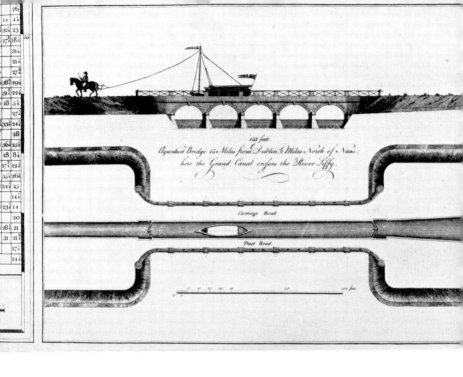

Page 34   The Leinster aqueduct over the Liffey: (*above*) from Alex Taylor's map
of County Kildare, 1783; (*below*) in 1896

as New Ross and Waterford. By this time the harbour* at James's Street had been completed and in 1786 Sir James Bond leased some ground from the canal company, extended the harbour and established a market there. The revenue from tolls amounted to £10,560 (Ir) in 1788.

The River Barrow between Monasterevan and Athy must have proved unsatisfactory as a navigation because of shoals and fluctuations in level and the company must have decided to continue the stillwater canal to Athy. When the records recommence in August 1789, this work was already in progress. Once again it was divided up into lots of about a mile which were taken on by different contractors; the construction of the bridges, locks and aqueducts was similarly undertaken by local contractors. Evans was the engineer in charge but he was increasingly in demand by other navigation companies and the directors informed him that they would have to have his undivided attention. He replied that he could not disengage himself from commitments at Ballyshannon and Newry and eventually he was dismissed in December 1789; he subsequently became engineer to the Royal Canal Company.[2]

William Rhodes and James Oates, assistant engineers, supervised the work for a time aided by Archibald Millar, promoted from overseer. By April 1790 Millar was in complete charge, since Oates was engaged in carrying out surveys and Rhodes had been withdrawn to Dublin to work on the Circular Line which had been commenced that year (see Chapter 3), and was dismissed a few months later. Millar's reports to the board were long and often amusing. An early report concluded with the words, 'I am much in want of shoes and have no money'. In April 1790 he wrote:

In obedience to your Orders and agreeably to my appointment I have been over the Works several times and have given general salutary facilitating instructions which I hope will soon have a good effect, along with proper Instructions the regular

* In Ireland the term 'harbour' is used on the inland waterways to denote a basin or lay-by.

C

supply of Money will I expect in a short time put a new face on the Athy Canal—the thirteen pence per day subsistence mentioned to the Labourers on the Works has opened the Countenance of every Workman on the Line—that will bring forward a great many more labourers to the Works.

In the same report he said that there were 3,944 men at work. Wages seem to have varied in different parts of the country; for example the *Hibernian Journal*, 11 June 1790, reported: 'The labourers on the Royal and Grand Canals, turned out for increased wages last week. It was found necessary to accede to their proposition; and they now receive seventeen pence per day.'

Millar's next report spoke of errors in some of the levels; parts of the canal would have to be deepened and the fall of two of the locks increased to allow depth of 5 ft on the Camac and Grattan aqueducts. Some landowners complained that the canal was not following the line valued by the jury. Mr Pilsworth tried to prevent the men working where the canal passed through his orchard and so Millar instructed them to remain there at Pilsworth's expense, which had the desired effect.

Some of the contractors were finding it difficult to complete their contracts on time. Millar said that more men would have to be employed, but the company turned down his request to provide the tools and equipment for the additional labour. This evoked an angry response:

> I have been at great pains to hold forth the only certain mode by way of salve for curing the disorders of your backward works and shatter'd Contractors. I beg leave to repeat that it is the only mode to save money both to the Company and those hard labouring and hard bargain'd Contractors . . .

Eventually the board agreed to provide half the required equipment.

Jessop visited the line in the summer of 1790 and reported that the mistakes had been rectified and that 'the several Works of the Canal (putting expense out of the Question) appear to be executed in a masterly way'. This was Jessop's first recorded visit since he had carried out the surveys in 1772. He must, however, have come over on at least one other occasion because in 1790 he said that he would spend two or three months in Ireland 'as formerly' and there is a brief reference to a report submitted by him in 1789. He was rapidly becoming one of the foremost canal engineers in England and his reports, which carried great weight with the board, are entered in full in the minutes.

Work continued through the winter and in January 1791 Millar reported, 'Xmas times and very little work—weather also bad—a few of the subtaskers may finish this week'. In March he suggested that the trade and passage boats could start to operate to Athy while the final work on the locks was being completed. The directors awarded him a gratuity of 50 guineas (Ir) 'as a token of their Approbation and Esteem' and he was transferred to Dublin to work on the Circular Line, but he did not remain long in the company's service. Some boats continued to use the river from Athy to Monasterevan to

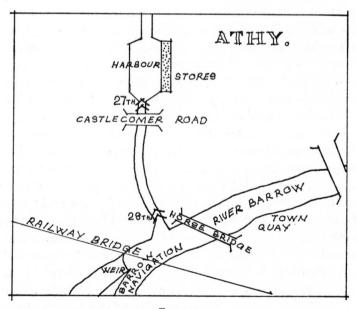

FIGURE 4

avoid the payment of tolls; it was possible to do this because the traffic had to lock down into the river and up again at Monasterevan. In 1802 it was reported that Mr Cassidy, a distiller in Monasterevan, had two boats on the river and in 1806 there is a reference to a lock, 40ft by 8ft, in the weir above the bridge at Athy, built by Mr Redshaw to preserve a greater head of water for his mill. This lock was said to be used about 500 times each year; a few of these boats went up to Monasterevan but most of them were drawing turf from Clonee bog, about 3 miles upstream of Athy, where there was a canal 4 miles long into the bog.

In 1789, with work well advanced on the Monasterevan to Athy Line, the directors turned their attention to the link with the Shannon. In that year a petition had been laid before the Irish Parliament for leave to construct another canal to the Shannon, north of Lough Ree; the surveys of the 'Royal' Line made in the 1750s were being used by the petitioners.[3] The story of the Royal Canal 'shoemaker' is well known. Samuel Smiles recounted how one of the directors of the Grand Canal Company, a 'retired shoemaker', conceiving himself to have been insulted by his colleagues, resigned from the board and vowed he would build a rival canal.[4] All the evidence points to John Binns as being the principal promoter of the Royal Canal scheme,[5] but there is no record that he had any connection with shoemaking and he remained a director of the Grand Canal Company until 1790, several months after the Royal Canal Company received its charter.[6] A study of the names of the directors of both companies in the 1780s reveals another name, William Cope, who was a member of the Grand Canal Company board for one year, 1784-5, attending nine meetings. He joined the Royal Canal board from the start and stayed until 1802, the same year in which John Binns also ceased to be a director. A Dublin directory records a wholesale silk merchants' in Dame Street called 'Cope & Binns' in the 1780s and a shoemaker called George Cope in Nicholas Street in 1818. It is just possible that William Cope influenced his more powerful friend to help him to establish the new company.

Faced with the threat of a rival, the Grand Canal directors made the very reasonable suggestion that the new canal should commence at Kinnegad, about 10 miles north of Edenderry, with a canal linking it with the Grand Canal. This would save an enormous amount of time and money and the two companies would have a mutual interest in the whole undertaking. The Royal Canal Company considered the proposal 'inexpedient' and it is interesting to note that John Binns was present when the reply from the Royal Canal Company was read. Some work had been carried out on a survey of the proposed junction canal but, following this rejection, the directors concentrated on the Shannon Line.

Some drainage work had been carried out in the bog west of Lowtown and now contracts were made to proceed with the construction work. Michael Hayes undertook to build the 19th lock, a small aqueduct and a tunnel under the canal for £2,000 (Ir), all the work to be completed by March 1791, and James McMahon contracted to carry out the earthwork from Lowtown to Ticknevin 'at 5 8s the running perch', banks and back drains included.

In 1789 the directors had asked William Chapman,[7] who was at that time in charge of the construction of the Naas Canal, to carry out a survey of a line from Lowtown to Ticknevin with an extension to Kinnegad. The second part was, as we have just seen, abandoned but Chapman's comments about the construction of canal through bog are very interesting:

The declining Surface of a Bog arises not from want of Cohesion but from the greater Desication of its Boundaries and from its small degree of Permeability to water with which the interior Part is surcharged and swoln up like a Sponge, which of course occasions its Convexity—the great Point therefore undoubtedly is, to have the Level of the Canal sufficiently below the Surface to allow for the Desication and consequent subsidence of the Bog, and what that Subsidence should be in all Cases, I conceive no difficult Matter to be ascertained which when done would be the Acquisition of one of the greatest Desiderata in the Science of Canals.

Chapman subsequently designed a 'cylindric implement of steel plate sharp at the lower edge' with which he was able to obtain samples of the bog at different levels, establish the water content and estimate the rate of subsidence.[8]

Chapman's comments do not agree with those set out by Smeaton in his second report to the company in 1775:

> Everything that I have done and seen in bog, even in moderate deep sinkings, has been attended with difficulty, and uncertain expenses, while, at the same time, where the level of the canal can be carried superficially upon bog, it is a thing perfectly easy. . . . The sinking a little at a time, as for instance, one spit of the spade annually, giving in the meantime leave for the water to drain off, and the adjacent bog to consolidate, is the best method I know of, and think, with much labour and patience, you may get ten or twelve feet deep. 'Drain the bog' say they that think it easy; true, this is a very effectual method, but then it is in this that all the difficulty consists. No drain can operate below the level of the water it contains, and by the same rule that you can make a drain a foot wide, and keep it open, you may make a canal of fifty feet wide and keep it open to the same depth. Avoid a bog if you can, but by all means possible, the going deep into it.[9]

Smeaton's views carried the most weight; the eventual result of adopting his plan was the construction of a canal on the same level as the original bog, but, because of the subsidence on either side of the canal, great embankments were required, which were to prove a constant source of trouble in the future.

It will be recalled that Jessop came over in 1790 to inspect the various works. Some progress had been made when he arrived and he set out his recommendations as to the best mode of proceeding. No centre drain was to be made but two drains were to be cut on either side of the centre line about two perches from it. Similar drains were to be made at 8 and 50 perches and, where the bog was very wet, transverse openings would be necessary. The drains were to be gradually deepened and widened. The outer edges of the two perch drains would ultimately form the verges of the canal. They were to be deepened in such a way as to leave a pyramidal core in the centre, which would prevent the bottom from rising until the canal was ready to be filled.

Bernard and M. B. Mullins gave a full description of the work in their paper already mentioned. They were very critical about the adoption of Smeaton's advice and said that the line chosen was through the centre of a deep basin 'the lowest tap practicable being fifteen feet above the adjacent river, the Boyne'. 'That which was expected to be an unusually cheap reach of canal in shallow cutting', they added, 'ended, after several years of unremitting labour and enormous expence, in the formation of a bank on either side, 45ft high for a distance of 80 perches, so that the canal with the carrying up of its sides and bottom to the required level, containing 6ft of water, was in the centre of a high embankment, having a base of fully 400ft.' The paper went on to describe how ramparts, about 4 perches square, were formed by the material excavated from the drains and transverse drains. When the material had dried out, it was wheeled to the embankments where it was firmly trampled and new ramparts were formed as the drains were deepened. As soon as the canal could be filled with water, great quantities of clay were boated to the area (probably from the Hill of Downings) to line the bottom and sides of the canal, to sole the trackways and to cover the whole surface of the banks to give them weight and strength. Many times it was suggested that the line should be abandoned and a new cut made, but because of the influence of Lord Downshire, the principal landowner in the area, 'an example has been furnished for the benefit of the engineering world, at least of an error of the gravest character having been carried to a successful termination'.

William Chapman visited the works in 1791 while engaged in carrying out surveys for the company on the continuation of the line to the Shannon. He said that it was very difficult to persuade the 'taskers' to leave in the centre core and he suggested that more use could be made of 'flats' on either side of the core to help to transport material. In their report to the company in 1792 the directors said that work was being carried on over a distance of 20 miles. Jessop visited Ireland that summer and he also warned against the premature removal of the core although he thought that 'in general the works are doing well'.

Captain William Evans, one of the directors, was in charge of the works at this time, and in 1796 it was resolved that he should be paid 'an annual gratuity of 200 guineas [Ir] for his extraordinary exertions but that this shall not be drawn into a precedent'. He resigned from the board shortly after this and remained in the company's service until 1805 when he retired because the board refused to accept his advice about bringing additional supplies to the summit level.

John Killaly, who had carried out some surveys for the company, joined the staff in 1794 at a salary of £150 (Ir) per annum. Two years later the directors praised his work and said that from being a 'mere measurer and surveyor' he had become the 'complete superintendent of all kinds of work', and in 1798 he became the company's engineer at a salary of £400 (Ir) per annum.

Jessop returned in the summer of 1794 and he halted the construction of the embankment in one place where he considered that the bog had not been sufficiently drained; he warned that the back drains must not be neglected. Early in 1796 the water was admitted to the level from Lowtown to the 20th lock at Ticknevin but in May Captain Evans sent in a very depressing report about the work west of Ticknevin:

> The Edenderry Bog has again got into a bad state since the rain, and that what we have done latterly has been of little use, as the Bog has sunk, cracked and given way as formerly, so much that I conceive it lost labour to persevere in wheeling Bog Stuff on the bad parts as when the Top weight is added, the bottom gives way.

Evans recommended that the water should be let into the canal to enable them to draw clay to make a puddle drain at about 40ft from the water's edge to help to confine the banks.

Jessop arrived in August and suggested a procedure which was to become a great source of controversy. In order to ensure the security of the banks he said that 3ft of water should be admitted into the canal and that clay should be boated to the site, which was causing trouble, where a 'Rib of Clay' should be constructed on both sides about 50ft from the verge of the canal. Trenches should be cut in lengths of a few yards to allow the wall of clay to sink down to the bottom of the bog. The wall should be 3yd thick at the base and should gradually be reduced and allowed to lean towards the canal to counteract the tendency of the bog to press outward and to have 'the effect of a battering wall'. Acting on this advice the canal was filled to a depth of 3ft in December. Fifty Irish guineas were added to Jessop's fee for that year 'as a small testimonial of the continuance of our esteem for him', giving him a total of £346 18s 9d (Ir) for that year.

Early in the new year, 1797, the canal was opened to Philipstown (Daingean) and it was anticipated that the line to Tullamore would be completed by the summer. Jessop was told that there would be no need for him to visit Ireland that year but, shortly after this, in August, a breach occurred where the wall of clay was being constructed. It took two months to repair and Jessop was asked to come over to inspect the embankments in November. Before he arrived, one of the directors, Richard Griffith, wrote to him in terms which must have displeased him. Griffith attacked his decision to fill the canal:

> I am therefore to acquaint you that I was convinced at the time and am now still more so by the event, that you were entirely wrong on that occasion, and I am persuaded that if you had seen the state of the Bog you would not have decided as you did.

Griffith went on to attribute the breach to four causes; the lack of lining in the canal, the fluid state of the banks, the want of attention to the back drains and:

lastly to a wall of clay built on the South Bank which having no other foundation than that on which the whole of this part of the Canal is erected, namely water . . . sunk down from its own weight, and in sinking displaced part of the base on which the Canal was erected, made cracks and fissures in the Banks, into which the water of the Canal rushed and carried away the whole body—This last circumstance I consider as the immediate operative cause of the Breach.

He considered that the wall of clay should be abandoned, the canal should be lined with clay and a mixture of clay and bog material should be added to the banks on a very broad base: 'it is admitted that the whole of this part of the Canal is afloat, and therefore I say that one broad and equal pressure is the true mode of preserving it . . .'.

Jessop replied that he could not agree; adding weight to the embankments would cause them to have a greater tendency to sink and crack and he strongly defended his wall of clay. He decided to come over in December and reported to the board that he still considered the wall of clay the best means of securing the banks, but he suggested that it should be moved to a distance of 75ft from the edge of the canal and should be constructed progressively, with gaps between each section gradually filled in to form a complete wall. Clay should be thrown into the canal wherever it had a disposition to rise as this would help to prevent the water seeping into the banks. He warned that the back drains must be kept open as effectively as possible:

for though it can never be drained below a certain Depth, and the Canal and Banks must ever float, like a huge Vessel upon an imperfect fluid below it, it is material that this Vessel should have the thickest possible bottom to it, and every inch that the Drains can be lowered will add an inch to its thickness. . . . I hope and trust that the combined effect of those several operations will give permanent stability to a work to which in all probability there is nothing similar in the world.

The promised opening to Tullamore was not long delayed. Two of the directors, Mr Irwin and Mr Marsh, visited the line in March 1798 and expressed pleasure in the progress. They reported that the wall of clay was being constructed with great perseverance at the place where the breach had occurred. By the summer Evans reported that the line to Tullamore was complete and he suggested that a harbour should be constructed there because, until a decision was reached about the line of the extension to the Shannon, Tullamore would be the terminus.

Then, in January 1800, another breach occurred at the same site and the controversy flared up again. Jonn Killaly was in charge of the repairs and he reported that he was filling in deep and numerous cracks and trampling and settling the bottom of the canal. He then proposed wheeling up bogstuff to raise the bottom of the canal, which he thought was too deep, and on top of this he intended to place a covering of clay. While he continued to support Jessop's wall of clay, he suggested that it should be moved back further from the canal.

Jessop visited Ireland in April in connection with a survey of a ship canal from Ringsend to Dunleary,[10] but he said that his engagements in England prevented him from visiting Edenderry. He did, however, discuss the matter in correspondence with the board. He said that from Killaly's report he concluded that the wall had not sunk down to the firm ground beneath the bog, as he had intended that it should, because the crust of firm bogstuff had proved thicker than anticipated. It would be necessary this time to sink the trenches to a sufficient depth to allow the clay to penetrate to firm ground.

The breach took many months to repair and, in the meantime, Griffith, convinced that the wall was at fault, did his best to halt the construction of it and suggested once again that Jessop should admit that he had made a mistake. He asserted that the discovery that the weight of the wall had not been sufficient to penetrate the crust proved that it would have been strong enough to support the canal and embankments. Killaly admitted that the wall was the immediate cause of the breach. He explained that it had penetrated through to the crust and remained stationary for some time; it was therefore thought to have reached firm ground. Some time later cracks had appeared; more clay had been applied, which had caused it to sink suddenly, and fresh cracks had formed which communicated with those in front, finally causing the breach. He dismissed as impractical a suggestion that the space on both sides of the canal should be filled with water and supported Jessop's plan to sink the wall to firm ground.

By this time Killaly had increased the inner slopes of the canal considerably and raised the bottom with large quantities of clay and he now reported that the embankments were in a state of apparent security. Acting on this report Jessop wrote:

> and therefore tho' I feel the strongest impression that a wall of Clay executed according to the true intention of it would be the most probable means of obtaining security, I feel myself no longer inclined to advise it until any further symptoms may make its security, in its present state doubtful . . .

The wall of clay was abandoned and except for some minor trouble, the canal remained staunch for many years, but it was to present further problems in the future.

Jessop returned to Ireland in 1801 to survey the Shannon Navigation and the extension of the Shannon Line. There was a little correspondence with him in 1802 about some small matters but, thereafter, his role as consultant engineer to the company ceased. In 1806 when he was in Ireland carrying out a survey for the Barrow Navigation Company, he declined an invitation to wait upon the board, replying that he must return to England 'as the wind is fair for me and I am very much straitened for time'.

A short branch canal to the town of Edenderry had been commenced in 1797, financed by Lord Downshire. When the repairs to the 1800 breach had been completed, James Brownrigg, his lordship's agent, appealed to the board to complete the canal and harbour while the men and materials were at hand, but the work was not completed until 1802.

While the canal was being pushed slowly across the bog towards Tullamore, discussions had been taking place about the route from there to the Shannon. Omer had intended to use the River Brosna as a navigation,[11] but Smeaton thought that it might not be suitable in places. In the early 1790s a number of surveys were carried out. Among these was one by William Chapman which proposed taking the canal on a high level without a lock to Birr, with a 4 mile branch dropping down into the Shannon at Banagher. Killaly and Oates had surveyed a scheme to continue the long level to the north-west to within 3 miles of Athlone with a branch to Lanesborough,[12] but the Royal Canal Company objected to this. In 1794 Jessop emphasised the necessity to reach a decision because work on the locks leading down into Tullamore was held up while the high level extension was considered. Eventually it was decided to lock down into Tullamore, but it was still uncertain where the canal would go from there.

Jessop carried out more detailed surveys in December 1797 and put forward two schemes. The first involved continuing the canal from Tullamore on the same level through Frankford with a flight of locks leading down to the Shannon at Banagher and a possible extension to Birr and Roscrea. The second scheme followed the valley of the Brosna but the flooded state of the country prevented him from deciding whether the river itself should be used.

The question was still unresolved in 1801 when the company became involved with the Directors-General of Inland Navigation on the subject.[13] The 1751 commissioners had been dissolved by an Act of 1787 which set up separate bodies of commissioners for specific navigations, but they had proved equally inefficient.[14] They were replaced by five directors-general in 1800 and £500,000 was made available to help them to try to complete some of the outstanding works.[15] It will be shown later that the company had protracted negotiations with them on various subjects. On this issue they were not prepared to accept the company's suggestion that they should pay the additional cost of the Frankford line which would serve a larger area of the country. In June 1801, therefore, 'upon the maturest deliberation', the board decided to proceed with the line by the valley of the Brosna.

Killaly soon discovered that it would be impractical to use the river and it was decided to construct a canal the whole distance of 22 miles, eight of which were through bog. He rented a house on the Cloughan road near the site of the proposed aqueduct over the Silver River and Jessop was asked to inspect the line he had laid out. Jessop reported that the line was 'very judiciously laid out', but thought that Killaly's estimates, amounting to £89,731 (Ir) were rather high. The final cost of the work was £146,276 (Ir) but, as will be seen, unforeseen difficulties arose. Jessop recommended that the contractors should not commence work on the bog sections until some drainage work had been done. It will be remembered that the drainage work and the construction of the canal had been carried out almost simultaneously on the earlier bog sections and Jessop urged the directors to use 'the System established by experience.'

The drainage of the bog began, and 21 contractors were engaged to carry out the remaining earthworks, the price varying from £3 to £12 (Ir) per perch according to the difficulty of the terrain. Michael Hayes undertook to carry out all the masonry work before September 1803 with a penalty clause of £2,000.

The directors had decided that it would be expedient to appoint a 'confidential person' to superintend the work and Richard Griffith, his position strengthened by his victory over Jessop, was asked to devote five days each month to this task, for which he was to receive a gratuity of £26 5s (Ir). Early in 1802 Griffith reported, 'There is no serious difficulty to encounter in this line, but the Bogs, and they are tremendous.' The back drains had to be constantly recut to keep them open and they were deepened as the verge drains on either side of the canal were deepened; 'the want of these precautions has frequently irritated Mr Jessop, who is not easily moved to anger, and it has cost us much time and many thousands of pounds to remedy.'

The two locks leading out into the Shannon from the harbour were made 8oft by 16ft by 6ft to conform with the locks on the Shannon navigation so that river boats could reach the proposed harbour. The foundation stone of the last lock was laid in the summer of 1802 and Griffith said, 'I observed the usual ceremonies on this occasion, considering it as an epoch of no small importance in the annals of the Grand Canal Company.'

Hayes was forced to appeal to the board for an increase in his contract price because he had been compelled to raise the wages of all his workmen; the most skilled men, the stonecutters, were now receiving £1 6s (Ir) per week. The directors agreed to an increase and offered him a bonus of 500 guineas (Ir) if the work was all completed by November 1803. The shareholders were told that the canal would be ready by this date and that over 3,000 men were working on the line.

Griffith reported delays in receiving the workers' wages. The current practice was to cut notes in half, the second halves not being sent until a receipt was received for the first consignment. Griffith suggested that one parcel could be sent by post and the other by passage boat to cut down the delay. The company had agreed to accept the notes of the Bank of Ireland and certain private bankers in Dublin in payment of tolls in 1797 and at the same time the company issued its own notes in values of one to ten guineas (Ir). These were given to the employees in payment of wages and bore interest payable on fixed dates.

In December 1802 Griffith reported that the work had been delayed by a 'combination among the masons for higher wages'; another report spoke of the 'unchecked spirit of combination among the artificers and workmen of every denomination'. Advertisements had appeared for men to cut canals in England offering about 6s (30p), half of this to be paid at the time and the balance at the completion of the job. The wage in Ireland was now about 3s (Ir) so the offer was sufficiently attractive to draw many labourers from Ireland.

Very little work was achieved during the severe winter

months and hot lime was used to try to make the masonry set more quickly. However, in the spring Griffith estimated that all the earthworks would be finished by August and, although some of the stonework would still have to be completed, the water could be admitted in September and the canal opened to traffic on 1 October. He recommended that work should be commenced on the harbour facilities: 'You have terminated your canal in a wild and unfrequented situation to which it is useless to open a navigation unless you provide shelter at the same time for men and merchandize.' He suggested that the directors should view the line before the introduction of the water, 'otherwise the uncommon exactness, permanence and Beauty with which every part of this great work has been executed, will be unknown to them'. An inspection was arranged for 15 September and it was agreed that Killaly should be presented with a silver cup and 200 gold guineas at the opening ceremony.

Griffith drew up a memorandum of suggestions for the opening ceremony. Four trade boats should be selected and named the *River Liffey*, the *River Barrow*, the *River Shannon* and the *River Suck*. The first two should set out from Dublin and Athy respectively with symbolic cargoes; imported articles from Dublin and coal from Athy. The *River Shannon* with a cargo of Killaloe slates and Lough Allen coal and the *River Suck* with cattle should proceed along the Shannon. They should all converge on Shannon Harbour for the opening ceremony and while the boats from Dublin and Athy descended into the river and the Shannon boats ascended into the canal 'there should be a Royal discharge of artillery' and a military band playing 'God Save the King' and 'Rule Britannia'.

The board accepted his suggestions and lengthy instructions were drawn up about the conveyance of the distinguished guests from Dublin.[16] Four passage boats were to leave Dublin on Sunday morning, 9 October, and travel to Tullamore that day. The guests would spend the night in the company's hotel and travel to Shannon Harbour for the ceremony on Monday,

Page 51 Lock-houses: (*above*) Grange mills, 12th lock, in 1897. On the left is an early house built by Omer; (*below*) an unusual house at 26th lock near Tullamore, 1971

Page 52 Across the bog: (*above*) fitting new tail gates to 20th lock, Ticknevin, 1971, the long level in the background; (*below*) Blundell aqueduct in 1894, looking towards the site of the 1797, 1800, 1855 and 1916 breaches

returning to Tullamore for further entertainment that night and back to Dublin on Tuesday.

On 28 September the board decided to postpone the ceremony until 25 October because the 'uncommon and almost unexampled drought of the present season' was making it difficult to raise the levels of the canal. The directors were, however, still in confident mood and added that 25 October would be a very suitable date 'being the anniversary of his Majesty's happy accession to the throne of these Realms'.

On 11 October Griffith reported that the 29th level was not staunch and the water would have to be run off to carry out repairs. On 19 October the directors dispatched an urgent message to Griffith and Killaly to ask if there was a reasonable degree of certainty that there would be enough water in the canal for the ceremony. No ceremony took place, however, and finally the board resolved that the boats prepared for it 'be no longer detained but be allowed to proceed on their usual duties and business'.

In November Killaly reported 'the truth is we are rather losing than gaining water . . . as the leakage and absorption in

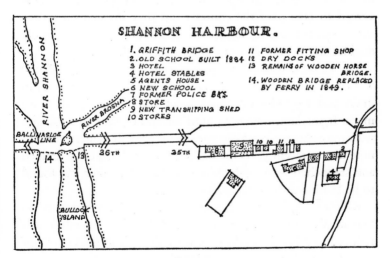

FIGURE 5

the Canal between Glyn and Belmont kept pace fully with the supply. You know, Sir, what a vast quantity of clay has been disposed of in the lining of this level.' Eventually, the Rahan level had to be drained again and new efforts made to staunch it. Killaly said that 50 perches had to be lined with 2ft 6in of well-puddled clay laid on furze. The floor of furze was laid 7oft wide extending 10ft under the foot of the banks on both sides of the canal. A lining of puddled clay was subsequently found necessary on the Glyn and Belmont levels.

In their report to the shareholders in February 1804 the directors explained that part of the canal had been found to pass through a 'rotten quarry' and although great care had been taken in lining the canal, the water had disappeared through swallow holes into subterranean passages connecting areas of bogland. They added that the canal was now open to trade and passage boats and in April Patrick Killeen, master of the *Ranger*, was presented with trousers and jackets for himself and his crew because his was the first boat from the Shannon to arrive in Dublin.

The death of Michael Hayes delayed the completion of some of the stonework and David Henry and Bernard Mullins agreed to take over the contract but they insisted on a time extension. It is interesting to see the gradual emergence of the engineering firm of Henry, Mullins & McMahon.

The canal continued to give trouble, and although Killaly was confident that it would eventually staunch itself, he had to drain and repuddle the Ballycowan and Rahan levels twice more. It was not, therefore, until the end of 1805 that the link with the Shannon was permanently secured. It is interesting to note that in recent years the Ballycowan level had to be drained and staunched with fresh puddle because the water was found to be leaking away into swallow holes.

Killaly's silver cup and gold guineas had been presented to him in May 1804 but, at his own suggestion, his salary was reduced to £630 (Ir) because of the reduction in the volume of work required of him. He continued to work for the company, carrying out surveys of various projects and investigating the position at the company's collieries. In 1810, after sixteen years with the company, he resigned to take up the position of engineer to the Directors-General of Inland Navigation, but, as will be seen, he continued to take an active interest in the company's affairs. He died on 6 April 1832 and there is a memorial to him in St Patrick's cathedral in Dublin, erected at the request of his widow, who died in 1837.

CHAPTER 3

The Company Expands

It has been seen what an enormous task the company undertook in completing the canal to the Barrow and the Shannon and it becomes an even more remarkable achievement in the light of the many other activities and problems which occupied the board during these years. In 1784 the construction of a link with the River Liffey had been discussed. Some of the directors felt that the Barrow and Shannon Lines should be completed first, but John Macartney, who had joined the board in 1783 and was a considerable shareholder, was anxious to carry out the work at the same time. Richard Griffith, who, as we have seen, was an influential director, supported him, and their view prevailed over the opposition led by Joseph Huband.[1]

The original plan, surveyed by John Brownrigg, which involved a direct descent by a series of locks into the Liffey from the harbour at James's Street, was abandoned and a more ambitious scheme was adopted. This was a canal nearly 4 miles long with seven locks following a circular route to join the Liffey further downstream, which had been surveyed by William Chapman.[2] Work commenced in 1790 and the level to Portobello without a lock was completed by the end of the year. Jessop inspected it when he visited Ireland in 1790 and recommended some small deviations in the line and in the positioning of the locks. He said that he feared that the entrance into the Liffey, at the mouth of the River Dodder, might be subject to silting, and in fact keeping the entrance clear was to prove a constant problem. He commented on the need for floating and graving docks in Dublin and suggested that the company should undertake this project.

Acting on this suggestion in 1791, when the canal was almost completed to Ringsend, the company petitioned Parliament for a grant to construct docks capable of accommodating 150 sea-going vessels.[3] The government granted £22,000 in 4 per cent debentures and stipulated that the docks should be completed by 1 November 1795.[4] Work was commenced with William Chapman acting as consultant engineer; in 1793 his brother, Edward, was appointed superintending engineer, a position which he held until the work was completed.

Some delays were experienced and Parliament agreed to extend the opening date. Finally in 1796 the docks were ready to receive the water and an official opening ceremony was planned for 23 April. It was organised on a lavish scale; tents, in which the guests were to take breakfast, were erected between the graving-docks, and the Lord Lieutenant, the Earl of

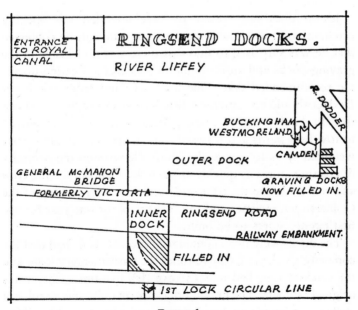

FIGURE 6

Camden, was invited to perform the opening ceremony. The viceregal yacht *Dorset* passed up through the entrance lock from the River Liffey followed by about twenty barges and pleasure yachts.[5] It was reported that there were over 1,000 guests and an estimated 150,000 people witnessed the scene; the courts rose to permit the judges and members of the Bar to attend.[6] The Lord Lieutenant was received by John Macartney, chairman of the company, whom he 'knighted on the spot'. DeLatocnaye, the well-known French traveller, was touring Ireland at the time and he described the scene:

> The Viceroy's yacht was the first to pass the gates to the sound of Volleys of cannon and when the centre of the dock was reached his lordship knighted, on the vessel, the contractor who had built and furnished part of the cost of this superb national work which completes on this side the junction of the canals with the sea. The Viceroy was afterwards rowed from one end of the dock to the other in an elegant barge, followed and preceded by the acclamations of the people.[7]

Jessop does not appear to have attended the opening ceremony but, when he came over that summer, he confessed that he was surprised to find that there was no leakage in the graving-docks and an insignificant leak in the floating-docks. He recommended that some loads of mud from the River Dodder should be scattered wherever leaks were suspected and that 'in windy weather a sailing Boat be frequently employed to tow backwards and forward some thorn bushes sufficiently weighted so as to agitate the Mud'. He stressed the necessity of erecting stores as quickly as possible to encourage the corn and coal trade and the company decided to offer free use of the Gollierstown quarries and toll-free travel for one year for the first twenty stores to be built.

The docks were not a commercial success. They had cost the company £112,149 (Ir), five times the parliamentary loan, and the Circular Line had cost £56,959 (Ir), five times Chapman's original estimate. The graving-docks were quite successful, but trade in the basin was disappointing and a bar caused by silting from the Dodder frequently restricted the size of vessels that could enter. An attempt was made in 1803 to persuade the government to take over the whole concern, but without success. Again in 1807, when the government was investigating the establishment of closed docks for the customs authorities, the board offered to sell the whole area for £100,000. The matter remained under discussion for several years but eventually the government decided to build the Custom House Docks on the north side of the river Liffey.[8]

There were three entrance locks. The new paddle wheel steamers were, however, too large for the locks and in 1839 the dockmaster reported that the bar was so bad that 'even those vessels of a moderate size cannot get into the docks'. Lengthy correspondence was carried on with the Corporation for Preserving and Improving the Port of Dublin, known as the Ballast Board, to determine whose responsibility it was to remove the mud, but it usually ended by the company having to do the work. On one occasion, in 1829, Hugh Pollen, the dockmaster, reported that the Camden tailgates had collapsed, 'the water at the entrance is much deeper than it has been for the last twenty years, I might safely say that it would require £400 to £500 to remove the quantity of mud that was removed'.

Figures are quoted of the number of vessels using the basin from 1811 until 1837. In 1812 the number had risen to 453 but in the 1830s the numbers fell away to an annual average of 200. It was pointed out that up to about 1826 the tonnage of most of the vessels was much larger (up to 400 tons) but that after that date the boats tended to be smaller. Hugh Pollen died in 1837 and was succeeded by Thomas Pollen, who proved very unsatisfactory, and, finally, in 1850, as will be shown in a later chapter, negotiations were commenced with a private group which was seeking a lease of the docks.

A branch that was considered at a very early stage was a line to Naas. Richard Evans had carried out a survey in 1782 and produced plans for a line with three docks, but, when no further action was taken by the company, a group of local landowners decided to raise a subscription to carry out the work. In 1786 an Act was passed setting up the County of Kildare Canal Company, empowered to construct a canal from the Grand Canal near Sallins via Naas towards Kilcullen.[9] William Chapman was engaged as engineer, his first appointment as a canal engineer,[10] and by 1788 the canal had reached Oldtown:

> This day was opened the new County of Kildare Canal. His Grace the Duke of Leinster and the other gentlemen of the Company were assembled this morning on board the *Milecent* packet, where an excellent breakfast, music etc., were provided. They proceeded with streamers flying, and the discharge of several pieces, from Sallins, up their own line through the Leinster and Wolfe Locks etc. On entering the new line, they were received with loud and repeated acclamations; and as soon as they entered the Leinster Lock, the populace seized the line, and drew them in triumph to the excavation of the third lock at Old Town.[11]

By 1789 the canal had reached Naas, a distance of $2\frac{1}{2}$ miles with five rising locks, but by this time the company was in financial difficulties. The total cost of the work had amounted to £10,477 (Ir), £5,000 (Ir) of which was owed to creditors. No further work was carried out and, despite another loan from the government, the debt stood at over £4,500 (Ir) by 1792. The Grand Canal Company directors had tried to help by granting toll remissions to enable trade to become established but they turned down an offer to take over the whole concern. The Kildare company had asked to have all its debts paid and to have half the value of the stock refunded to the subscribers, which would have amounted to an outlay of over £8,000. A counter proposal from the Grand Canal Company to make a loan available was rejected and the company struggled on.

In 1808 the Grand Canal Company purchased the canal through the Court of Chancery for £2,250 (Ir). It had not carried much traffic and by this time had fallen into a bad state of repair. It is interesting that Chapman had been asked by the

Kildare directors to try to preserve the angle of the roads crossing the canal and so had designed skew bridges which he claimed were the earliest ever constructed.[12] Unfortunately these bridges were lower than the Grand ones and did not have towpaths under them; so in 1808 the Grand Canal Company decided to replace them by conventional bridges and to lengthen the locks to conform with the main line. In addition to restoring the navigation the company decided to continue the canal to Corbally, a distance of 5¼ miles without a lock. All this work, which cost £20,291 (Ir), was completed by 1810, the contractors being David Henry, Bernard Mullins and John McMahon. It was intended to continue the line through Kilcullen and Baltinglass into County Wicklow and Killaly surveyed a route but nothing came of this scheme.

The Grand Canal Company had extended the passage boat service to Naas for a short period in the 1790s but it did not prove profitable. In 1811 the directors agreed to subsidise a service operated by Benjamin Lister but he withdrew it after one year because he said that the subsidy of £1 10s (Ir) per week was insufficient and the company refused to raise it. Trade was never extensive; in 1829 the locks were reported to be much out of repair and covered with weeds. At that time Christopher Farrell was the only trader. In the 1840s about 5,000 tons a year were carried on the canal, principally coal to Naas and flour from the Leinster mills at the 2nd lock on the return journey to Dublin. Mr Harrington, 'an extensive malster', commenced a carrying trade in 1848 and was allowed a reduced toll by the company but he ceased to operate the following year. As will be shown in a later chapter, the company decided at this juncture to enter the carrying business and Naas was one of the stations chosen for the experiment.

In addition to the construction of the Barrow, Shannon and Circular Lines, the company had to carry out some reconstruction and maintenance to the existing line. In 1787 and again in 1793 the canal was closed for several months for general repairs. There was another lengthy closure in 1804–5; while efforts were

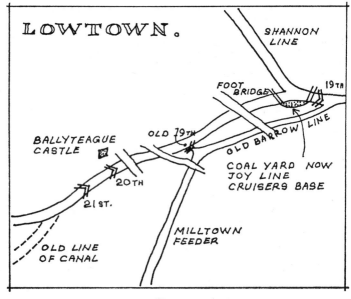

FIGURE 7

being made to staunch the canal between Tullamore and Shannon Harbour, the 3rd and 4th locks were rebuilt and the depth throughout the canal improved. The new stretch of canal at Ballyteague bog was incorporated during the closure, as was another short length of parallel canal at Lowtown. This had been constructed to economise in water and connected the Shannon and Barrow Lines below the summit level. Boats to and from Dublin continued to use the old Barrow Line until the 1860s, but as it was suggested that they were slipping through Lowtown by night to avoid the payment of tolls, the 19th lock, Barrow Line, was closed and all boats had to lock through the 19th lock at Lowtown.[13]

Huband Harbour, a small harbour on the Circular Line at Dolphin's Barn, was constructed in 1805 to accommodate idle boats. The Society of Friends acquired the excavated material for their new burial ground at Cork Street. This harbour, which was not filled in until recent years, became the last resting place of many old boats which were periodically sold off for breaking up.

After some years it had been found that the large court of directors and numerous committees were too unwieldy and they were replaced by a board of fifteen directors. For the next 30 years, until 1810, the company was controlled by a small group led by John Macartney and Richard Griffith. Macartney was not very popular in some circles; there is an interesting attack on him in the *Freeman's Journal* on 2 July 1791, five years before he received his knighthood:

> That learned ornament of the law, the *vice-admiral* of the dung boats, Mr Macartney. We recollect this northern luminary *before he rose*, and without pretending to divine in what quarter he will set, we trust that he will keep his lights to himself.

Richard Griffith, who joined the board in 1784, had made his fortune in early life trading in the West Indies; returning to Ireland, he settled at Millicent near Naas. He was a member of the Irish Parliament from 1783–90. His son, Richard, became an eminent engineer, particularly in the field of mining, and was knighted in 1858 for his work as a Commissioner of Valuation and chairman of the Board of Works.

Joseph Huband, a lawyer, was another influential director. He ornamented, at his own expense, the bridge which was to bear his name on the Circular Line. Other men who were active members of the board in this period were the Hon and Reverend J. Pomeroy (son of Lord Harberton), who was vicar of St Ann's, Dawson Street and an active member of the Royal Dublin Society, Arthur Chichester Macartney, Humphrey Hartley, J. B. Scriven, Turner Camac, George Maquay, Colonel Charles Eustace and two Dublin bankers, Benjamin Ball and William D. LaTouche.

Richard Baggs, the secretary, resigned in 1790, as did his successor, William Browne, after one year. From 1791 to 1804 William Greene, a former collector of tolls, was secretary at an annual salary of £110 (Ir) and he was succeeded by Daniel

Bagot. The company had moved from the Grafton Street premises to 32 Dawson Street in 1794 where meetings were held twice a week and subsequently three times each week.

The financial position of the company gradually worsened and the debt increased as new loans had to be negotiated.[14] No dividend had been paid in the early years, except a very small one in 1784 from pipewater revenue. In 1788, however, despite the enormous debt, a dividend of 1 per cent was declared and this was gradually increased until by 1793 it had reached 5 per cent. An attempt to raise money by a lottery in 1773 had been defeated by members of Dublin Corporation, who feared that it might interfere with their lottery to raise money for their new City Hall.[15] Another attempt to raise funds in 1791 was attacked by the *Freeman's Journal*:

> Would the most swindling lottery broker offer such a scheme, grounded on a chance of 197 to one. Our correspondent promises to shew this scheme in its true colours, and mark what shall appear to outdo the South Sea bubble, the bottle conjuror, the bank of Air, the lottery calculator and his black cats, or any other humbug heretofore attempted on public credulity.[16]

In the 1790s the government authorised further loans,[17] and Grand Canal stock, which had stood at 150 in 1792, fell to 104 in 1796. It is hard to see how the directors could justify the continued payment of dividends. The revenues of the company were increasing steadily, rising to £29,041 (Ir) in 1796, but set against the expenditure for that year this showed a big deficit:

	£ (Ir)
New works	73,094
Establishment	6,756
Interest on debt	17,388
Payment of dividend	16,220
	113,458

In 1800 the government decided to carry out an investigation of existing waterways and to examine the administration

GRAND CANAL-HOUSE, 23rd *October*, 1804.

AT a Meeting of the Court of Directors for the ordering,—managing, and directing the Affairs of the Company of Undertakers of the Grand Canal,

JOHN BARCLAY SCRIVEN, Esq. in the Chair:

ORDERED,

THAT on and from the 1st Day of *November* next, the GATE-KEEPERS of the several *Turnpike Gates*, on the Banks of the *Grand Canal*, do, until further Order, demand and receive the following Rates, in Lieu of those settled on the 31st of *August*, 1802, *viz.* —

		£	s.	d.
I.	A Coach drawn by four or more Horses,	0	1	4
II.	A Chaise drawn by four or more Horses,	0	1	1
III.	A Coach drawn by two Horses,	0	0	10
IV.	A Chaise drawn by two Horses,	0	0	6h
V.	A Gig, Chaise, or Jaunting Car,	0	0	4
VI.	A Waggon,	0	2	6
VII.	A Cart, or Car, drawn by more than one Horse, or other Beast, and carrying Stones, Bricks, Sand or Manure,	0	2	2
VIII.	A Cart, or Car, drawn by more than one Horse, or other Beast, and carrying any Article except Stones, Bricks, Sand or Manure,	0	1	1
IX.	A Cart, or Car, drawn by only one Horse, or other Beast, and carrying Stones, Bricks, Sand or Manure,	0	1	1
X.	A Cart, or Car, drawn by only one Horse, or other Beast, and carrying any Article, except Stones, Bricks, Sand or Manure,	0	0	6h
XI.	An Ox, or Cow,	0	0	3
XII.	An Horse, Mule or Ass,	0	0	1
XIII.	Calves, Sheep, Lambs, Goats and Hogs, *per Score*, and at the same Rate for a less Number,	0	0	10

The said Rates to be paid only at one Gate, and once in the same Day, in the same County.

By Order,

DANIEL BAGOT, *Secretary*

FIGURE 8. A minor source of revenue

of public funds for inland navigations,[18] one that resulted, as already mentioned, in the establishment of the Directors-General of Inland Navigation. In the course of this inquiry the Grand Canal Company revealed that its debt had now risen to £953,379 (Ir) and lengthy negotiations commenced with the directors-general about the sale of some of the company's tolls.[19] It was suggested that there should be a reduction from 3d (Ir) to 1d (Ir) per ton per mile, but no agreement was reached about the amount of compensation the canal company should receive. Negotiations were in progress at the same time about how much payment the company should receive for work on the middle Shannon but, although the directors-general tried to use this other issue to make a bargain, the canal company insisted that it was a separate question. No decision was reached and the discussion was reopened in 1805. The Grand Canal Board complained that the Royal Canal Company had been paid £95,866 (Ir) for a reduction from 1½d (Ir) to 1d (Ir) and in the light of this the offer of £130,000 (Ir) to reduce from 3d (Ir) to 1d (Ir) was insufficient; it was suggested that by aiding other navigation companies in this way the directors-general were trying to force the canal company to reduce its tolls without adequate compensation. The controversy continued but no agreement was reached.

It will be recalled that Dublin Corporation had agreed to pay the canal company 10 per cent of the gross pipewater rents. Relations became very strained; the corporation was frequently behind with its payments and was quick to complain if water was scarce in time of drought. In 1802 the corporation tried to slip some legislation through which would enable it to increase its charges without passing on the increase to the canal company. The latter managed to prevent this and then the corporation requested that the agreement to supply water should be annulled from 24 June 1804.[20] The canal company agreed but said that over £42,000 (Ir) compensation was due because the company had incurred this additional expenditure to ensure a guaranteed supply to the city basin. The corporation refused to pay and, in the meantime, the supply was terminated on the specified date. The corporation now tried to draw sufficient supplies from the River Dodder, which had contributed less than one-fifth of the water to the city basin, and began negotiations with the Royal Canal Company but, with the dry summer months, water soon became very scarce in the city. The company refused to negotiate a temporary agreement, pointing out that it now intended to sell the surplus water at its proper value.

The people of Dublin were very concerned about the threat to their water supplies and the newspapers attacked the company: 'The Grand Canal Directors are such good fellows, that they wish not to allow the Citizens of Dublin to drink water, and strive to keep it out of their way. What good-natured folks —they deserve well of the people of Dublin and closely watch their waters.'[21] The directors tried to defend themselves and published a notice claiming that they had adhered to the agreement with 'the most scrupulous and inviolable fidelity', despite the low returns.[22] In answer to the corporation's accusation that the water was being taken from the city basin to supply the canal, the directors retorted: 'Unless the Pipe-water Committee or their engineers have discovered some new method of making water flow up an ascent, any supply from the City Bason to the canal would answer no other purpose than to enable children for their diversion to paddle between the City Bason and first lock.' Finally the company said that if the compensation was not paid by 1 August the surplus water would be sold to the highest bidder.

Eventually two members of each side met and the company sent a letter to the Lord Lieutenant stating its final terms in the matter. 'Out of commiseration for their fellow citizens' the company was prepared to make a considerable abatement 'to prevent as far as may be within their power the effects which they are apprehensive might result from the further use of Dodder water'. The terms offered were that the company should receive 15 per cent of the gross water rents for 61 years and the corporation should have the right to withdraw the north city from the agreement if a supply was obtained from the Royal Canal in the future. The corporation refused these terms, though by this time it was September and the shortage of water in the city was acute. The Lord Lieutenant appealed to the company to restore the supply, 'the actual suffering from the want of water has already been considerable and the apprehension not only of the scarcity being increased but of the calamity which may be produced by infectious diseases and by other obvious causes has excited a very general and alarming sensation'. The basin was filled, the directors leaving 'the just rights of the Grand Canal Company under the Honourable protection of his Majesty's Government on which they place the firmest reliance'.

Negotiations recommenced but, with the water restored, the matter dragged on and it was not until 31 May 1805 that an agreement was sealed. The company was to receive 12½ per cent if the whole city was supplied and 15 per cent if the supply was restricted to the south city; the agreement was to operate for 61 years and the claim for compensation was withdrawn. This produced an income of about £2,000 for the company, which was reduced to about £1,500 when the Royal Canal Company commenced a supply to the north city.

The prevention of bathing and 'swimming dogs' in the Circular Line was always a difficult problem and prosecutions were made from time to time. Efforts were also made to prevent the dumping of rubbish in the canal; for example in 1818 it was reported that 'a mattrass and Bedding were immersed in the Canal at Portobello Barrack'. It is interesting that as early as 1821 there were reports of small boys throwing stones at the passengers from the city bridges. In 1845 there was a suggestion that the water was 'unwholesome and unfit for domestic use' and Dr James Apjohn was paid a fee of £21 to carry out an analysis. He reported that it was 'soft, sweet and wholesome and well adapted for domestic use of every description'. In the 1860s, as it will be shown in a later chapter, new arrangements

Page 69 Harbours: (*above*) Tullamore in 1894. The warehouses in the background have since been demolished; (*below*) Edenderry in 1971, on the short branch financed by Lord Downshire

Page 70 Harbours: (*above*) James's Street, Dublin, in 1969. The house with the porch was formerly the general manager's; (*below*) Athy in 1897

were made to cope with the increasing demand for water in the city.

The military continued to make use of the canal for the movement of troops and early in 1797 the company, appreciating the role the canal could play during the unsettled state of the country and the threat of a French invasion, wrote to the government pointing out that parliamentary assistance with canal building would hasten the provision of an important line of communication between Dublin and the rest of the country, but the suggestion did not meet with any response. A corps of yeomanry of canal employees and local farmers around Edenderry was raised to 'supress defenderism and preserve the public peace', and a similar body was raised in Dublin with William Greene, the secretary, as captain. In 1796 a blunderbuss and a case of pistols were purchased for each of the passage boats and, in 1812, to cater for the growing fleet, three more blunderbusses and six pistols were obtained second-hand for £12 (Ir).

The canal was closed by the rebellion in June 1798; the military used it as a line of defence to protect the city and the bridges were barricaded. The company placed its boats and officers at the disposal of the army. A small amount of damage occurred along the line of the canal but traffic was resumed again by the end of July. When announcing the resumption of traffic, the company assured the public that there would be armed guards on the passage boats and troops stationed along the canal. The canal was used to convey the troops part of the way to join battle with the French invaders at Ballinamuck and French prisoners were brought to Dublin by water after the battle.[23]

Troops continued to guard the canal and passage boats for many years; the number varied according to the state of the country and it was some years before the barricades were removed from the bridges. In 1804 the company tried to persuade the authorities to pay a fixed sum each year to enable boats to be held in readiness for them at all times. This was refused and

E

GRAND CANAL.

Two Hundred Pounds, Reward.

WHEREAS the East Bank of that Part of the Grand Canal, leading to Edenderry, was, on the Night of Saturday, the 29th Day of February last, maliciously and feloniously cut across, by some evil-minded Persons unknown:

AND WHEREAS a Breach was, in like Manner, made in Part of the South Bank of the said Canal, at Tubberdaly, on the Night of Sunday, the first Day of March Instant; which Breach was enlarged, on the Morning of the 2nd Instant.

AND WHEREAS, several other wilful and malicious Attempts, to injure the Canal, and to obstruct the Navigation thereof, have been made by (among other Things) cutting the Banks—damaging the Locks, Lock-Gates, and Sluices—and by throwing the Stones off some of the Bridges and Trackways into the Canal.

Now, the Court of Directors of the Grand Canal Company, in Order to prevent the Repetition of such Outrages, do hereby offer A REWARD OF TWO HUNDRED POUNDS Sterling, to any Person who shall discover and prosecute to Conviction, within six Calendar Months from the Date hereof, any one or more of the Persons concerned in any of the said Offences; and, if any Person will give such Private Information, to any Magistrate, or to any of the Company's Officers, as will lead to the Apprehension and Conviction of any one or more of the Persons concerned therein, such Person shall be entitled to a Reward of Fifty Pounds.

Dated this 11th Day of March, 1812.

By Order,

DANIEL BAGOT, *Sec.*

His Grace the Lord Lieutenant is pleased to promise His Majesty's free Pardon to any one of the Persons concerned, who shall within six Months first discover his Accomplices, so that they, or any of them be apprehended and convicted of the said Offence.

By His Grace's Command,

CHARLES SAXTON.

Dublin : Printed by William Porter, Grafton-street, Printer and Stationer to the Grand Canal Company.

FIGURE 9. Malicious damage

the company said that it could not guarantee boats at short notice in future, but the military continued to make use of the special rates allowed by the company for the movement of troops and their baggage.

In addition to the expansion of the passage boat services, trade on the canal was increasing steadily as it was extended south and west of Dublin. It became necessary to increase supervision to prevent 'illicit practices' and a 'comptroller of trade' was appointed at the 1st lock to carry out checks on cargoes and record the destinations of the boats. He was provided with a boring iron for searching boats and fines were imposed for evasion of tolls; for example, a fine of £5 (Ir) was imposed for concealing oats under a load of dung, because the latter was subject to a lower toll. Half the fine was paid to the person who detected the fraud.

In 1798 the toll on corn, meal, flour, malt and most other merchandise was increased to 3d (Ir) per ton per mile, but turf, building materials and dung were excluded from this increase. Drawbacks were paid on goods from distant places, such as Clonmel on the River Suir, and refunds were also made if the trade was hindered by stoppages such as deficiency of water. A breakdown of tonnage for the year ending February 1801 shows that out of the total of 110,855 tons carried on the canal, nearly three times as many goods were shipped into Dublin as outwards from the city.[24] Flour, turf and building materials were the principal commodities entering the city and manure and general merchandise the principal exports. By 1810 the tonnage had risen to 205,435 tons, over 80,000 tons of which was being handled through Portobello, and the revenue of the company had risen from £29,041 (Ir) in 1796 to £84,335 (Ir) in that year.[25]

In 1803 an attempt was made to encourage traffic in cattle, sheep and pigs; the board hired a boat to the Farming Reposi-tory, offering them a special low toll of ½d (Ir) per ton per mile on condition that they limited their freights to certain fixed rates. The business was not conducted in a very satisfactory manner, they were soon heavily in debt to the company and the scheme was abandoned. A limited trade in livestock did develop, but it was never very significant because of the prob-lem of cleaning the boats if they were not exclusively used for the carriage of animals.

In 1804 Richard Griffith delivered a long memorandum to the board, attributing the slow development of trade to the lack of organisation among the traders which produced un-necessary delays and high freight rates. He submitted a plan, which was approved by the board, that the company should build additional stores at Shannon Harbour and that twelve new trade boats should be financed by the company which he would lease and gradually refund the cost. Some of the stores and boats were built, but it is not clear whether Griffith commenced to trade as a carrier although a boat referred to as 'Mr Griffith's boat' was reported to have sunk on Lough Derg in 1808.

A system was adopted of having a director available at James's Street Harbour once a week to hear complaints and investigate irregularities. One report had stated that there were 'numberless improprieties committed on the canal'. Thomas Oldham established himself as a broker at the harbour and the company guaranteed him an income of £200 (Ir) per annum over and above the rent of stores. In 1808 it was decided to appoint a 'Superintendent of Trade' whose first task would be an investigation of the conduct and capabilities of the several collectors who had been established at various stations on the line. Andrew Bagot, a clerk in the secretary's office who had shown an interest in the development of trade on the canal, was appointed to this position.

Key to FIGURE 10 on page 73 opposite

1	Caretaker's house	19	Middle harbour filled in 1960
2	Offices and Boardroom		
3	Cashier's house	20	Inwards store
4	General manager's house	21	Ballinasloe store
		22	Inner harbour filled in 1960
5	Chief clerk's house		
6	Chief accountant's house	23	Turf bank
		24	Guinness laboratory and store
7	Engineer's house		
8	Goods agent	25	Carpenter's shop and saw mill
9	Store formerly police barracks		
		26	Former passage-boat quay and bell
10	Foreman carpenter's house		
		27	Storekeeper's office and store
11	Storekeeper's house		
12	Three dry docks	28	Store with paint loft and cover maker's loft
13	Shipwright's shop		
14	Store leased to D. E. Williams	29	Forge
		30	Cover shed
15	Rupee bridge	31	Harness maker
16	Bond harbour with Guinness malt store in 1885; subsequently all filled in	32	Fitting shop
		33	Stables
		34	Hay shed
		35	Stables
17	Sugar store in later years	36	Horsing superintendent's house
18	Limerick store		

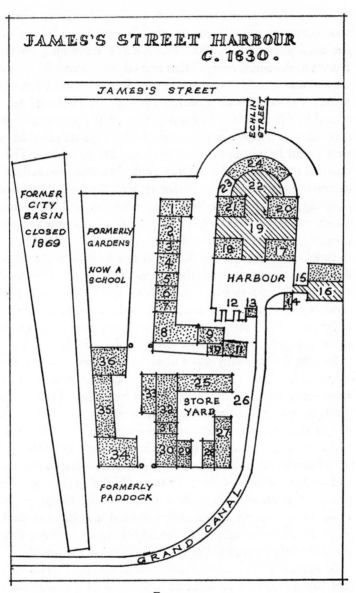

FIGURE 10

By this time, in addition to the small traders, several firms were operating quite large concerns. The principal traders on the canal were Hyland, Pim, Duggan and Berry and, on the Shannon, Palmer, Going, Dillon and Glynn. Messrs Berry had commenced to trade in 1806 and soon leased stores at James's Street, Tullamore and Shannon Harbour. A memorial submitted by them in 1812 in connection with the payment of an account which they owed to the canal company, provides a very useful insight into the system used by the traders. They said that they had conducted their trade 'in a more spirited and extensive manner' than any other trader; they had introduced hatching, locking and sealing boats, weighing and examining goods on receipt and delivery, giving regular receipts for cargoes, taking samples out of spirits and measuring the depth of casks. A resident partner looked after the business at each of the three centres and all their employees were of a good character. By introducing 'scotch drays and large spokewheel cars' they had greatly increased their trade in flour from places as far away as Galway. These high standards must have helped to encourage other traders to follow their example.

In 1809 the company was forced to raise further loans, but despite this a dividend of 6 per cent was declared. Although the revenues of the company were steadily increasing, the financial position was not improving. The company was plunging deeper and deeper into debt and the assurance of the directors that there would be a rapid increase in prosperity when the war with France ended did not satisfy the shareholders; in fact the end of hostilities was destined to mark the beginning of a period of depression in trade throughout the kingdom. In 1809, therefore, the shareholders formed a committee and, when the directors refused to pay any attention to them, they decided to try to vote the existing directors off the board.

In February 1810 many heads rolled. Sir John Macartney had already withdrawn from an active role in the company's affairs and now Richard Griffith, Benjamin Ball, Humphrey Hartley, A. C. Macartney and some of their supporters were deposed by the 'largest meeting of Proprietors that ever assembled'. The Rev Pomeroy and Joseph Huband survived together with Lord Cloncurry and M. J. Plunkett who had recently joined the board. The new men, who now assumed control of the company, were Nicholas Fanning, Thomas McKenny, who as Lord Mayor of Dublin was later to receive a knighthood, William Hutton, a distiller, and two lawyers, James Hamilton and Beresford Burston.

The new board set about a programme of retrenchments and reorganisation which produced a saving of about £5,000 (Ir) per year, but the annual dividend of 5 per cent was maintained. Negotiations were commenced again with the directors-general about the sale of part of the company's tolls. The directors suggested a reduction in the toll from 3d (Ir) to 1½d (Ir) per ton per mile for a payment of £313,800 (Ir), which represented thirty years purchase based on the tolls for 1809, but they were prepared to accept the sum of £205,710 (Ir), based on the figures for 1810, which was a bad year, if the Royal Canal rates were raised to 1½d (Ir), thus placing the two companies on an equal footing:

> In a word—wanting money—confessing this want—we hereby solicit at your hands either an acceptance of our terms if you deem them reasonable; or if not, that you will discuss their Justice, and state your objections, or lastly that you will favour us with a Counter Proposal on your part . . .

At the same time 'amicable discussions' were held with the Royal Canal Company for the first time since the formation of the rival company. It was agreed by the Royal directors that they would raise their tolls to 1½d (Ir) if the directors-general accepted the Grand proposals. It was further suggested that the government should be asked to help both companies to reduce their debts, 'the prosperity of one company would promote the prosperity of the other as well as that of the United Kingdom and no competition could exist between them except in performing good offices the one towards the other'. The Royal

Canal had not yet been completed to the Shannon and the Grand directors suggested that the line should follow a northerly route, with a canal linking the two systems between Edenderry and Thomastown. These suggestions were not very well received and friendly relations were soon at an end. Word reached the Grand directors that the Royal Canal Company had put forward proposals to the directors-general that the canal should join the River Inny and thus enter the Shannon at Lough Ree, and battle was joined once more.

The whole question of what line the Royal Canal should follow and the grave financial difficulties of the two companies seemed to warrant government intervention and a full investigation was ordered. The Grand Canal Company at first refused to co-operate, but the financial position of the company was so grave that eventually the board agreed to disclose the details required.[26] Many interesting statistics were prepared for this inquiry; for example it was shown that the capital cost of the canal system had been high:[27]

		£ (Ir)
Expended prior to 1772		79,816
Dublin to Athy		406,783*
Lowtown to Tullamore	£ (Ir)	
construction	175,565	
Edenderry branch	692	
Breach repairs, 1797, 1800	12,208	
	——	188,465
Tullamore to Shannon Harbour		146,276
General Repair, 1804–5		25,441
Circular line		56,959
Ringsend docks		122,149
Naas and Corbally line	£ (Ir)	
expended by Kildare Company	10,477	
Corbally extension	20,291	
	——	30,768
		£1,056,657

* It is not clear whether this figure includes the pre-1772 expenditure.

Since the formation of the company in 1772, parliamentary assistance had amounted to £93,259 (Ir) (most of it by way of 4 per cent debentures),[28] stock to the value of £571,950 (Ir) had been created and £968,000 (Ir) had been raised in loans at 4 and 6 per cent.[29] The continued payment of a high dividend and the interest on the debt, which had increased rapidly as new loans were negotiated, together with the cost of the establishment, far exceeded the annual revenue; in 1810 this deficit amounted to £38,084 (Ir).

The directors, meanwhile, continued their efforts to improve the financial position of the company. They managed to turn the large deficit of 1810 into a profit of £5,164 (Ir) in the year ending February 1812. As a result of the government inquiry the Royal Canal Company was deprived of its charter, the directors-general assumed responsibility for completing the canal and the New Royal Canal Company was subsequently incorporated to administer it.[30] The Grand Canal Company, with its increasing financial stability, fared much better. A grant of £150,000 was authorised to help liquidate the debt but it was subject to certain conditions. The most important of these were that in future no dividend was to be declared except out of clear profits, the company had to add a sum equal to one-third of the grant towards the liquidation of the debt, a sinking fund of £30,000 had to be established and the profits from the collieries had to be used to reduce the debt. The shareholders, who had been receiving a dividend of 5 or 6 per cent since 1800, did not like these conditions and three special meetings of the company had to be held before the directors could persuade them to accept these terms, which were the best that could be negotiated. Trade on the canal was prospering; in 1812 the tonnage increased to 231,112 and, with the easing of the financial burden as a result of the suspension of dividends and the reduction in annual interest on the debt, the company seemed to be entering a more successful phase.

CHAPTER 4

Troubled Years and New Branches

IT was inevitable that the troubled state of the country during the war with Napoleon would eventually result in damage to the canal works. In March 1812 James Brownrigg, Lord Downshire's agent at Edenderry, reported that two breaches had been made in the Edenderry branch canal. These were quickly repaired but his report contained a warning of the possibility of further trouble:

> The lower classes seem to be in a state of ferment under an apprehension for which I fear there is too much grounds that the provisions is going so fast out of the country that a scarcity must ensue and I apprehend it is to this cause the outrage is owing.

This was followed by a letter from Lord Cloncurry,[1] one of the directors, written on 10 March from his home at Lyons, near the 13th lock:

> I am sorry to tell you that some mischief was done in the neighbourhood last night several of the Coping stones and part of the trackway of Henry Bridge being thrown into the Canal—I had unfortunately gone from home in the hope of doing some good in the direction of Tullamore or I daresay the thing would not have occurred. The directors may be very certain that I shall make every exertion in my power to discover and punish the stupid authors of this mischief for certainly whatever the effect the canal may have further from Dublin it does not raise the price of provisions in this neighbourhood.

He went on to say that two boats had been raided by a mob at Philipstown (Daingean) and their cargo of potatoes sold at 4d (Ir) per stone, and he stressed the need for more military guards along the canal. The company's engineer confirmed this attack and said that the mob was directed by a 'fellow stiling himself Captain Fearnought or Firebrand'. He added that the military stood by and would not act without a warrant from the magistrate who, although he was at home, refused to come out.

Soon reports began to come in of breaches and damage to locks and bridges. More boats were plundered of oatmeal and potatoes and Mr Hulbert, the collector at Monasterevan, was warned, 'You must not sign a Pass for any boat that has potatoes in it over two sacks or if you do we will cut your lock gates. Signed John the Carder.'

A special committee of five directors set off to view the line and were joined by Lord Cloncurry when they reached Lyons. Their report contains this comment:

> Your committee feel that no actual want of provisions in the Country has been the real cause of those Acts of Violence— that an artificial want appeared in some of the towns on your Line owing to the speculations of Individuals who purchased potatoes and oatmeal for the advanced market of Dublin to- gether with the improper conduct on the sale of provisions by Forestallers in those towns . . .

New military posts were set up and the number of troops along the line was greatly increased. By the end of March the directors were able to report to the shareholders that, while trade had been interrupted for a short period, there had been no material damage done to the works. John Stokes, the acting engineer, was given a gratuity of £50 (Ir) for his 'zeal and extraordinary exertions' in connection with the repairs. It will be recalled that John Killaly had left the company in 1810 and John Stokes, who had joined the company in 1804 as super- visor of works, was promoted acting engineer in 1812. His ap- pointment was confirmed three years later but without any increase in his salary of £300 (Ir) per annum. He had eleven children and frequently appealed to the board for an increase in salary but, although he was given gratuities from time to time, he was still receiving the same wage when he died in 1843.

The end of hostilities with France brought a decline in trade and in 1815 a group of disgruntled shareholders sent a requisition to the board for a special meeting, 'fully sensible that the present very embarrassed state of the Company's affairs is the consequence of the mode in which they have been formerly managed'. The board refused to comply with the requisition but a committee was set up to investigate the recession in trade. The shareholders continued to press for a meeting and enlarged their criticisms of the way in which the company was being managed. Finally a meeting was held at which Sir William Cusack Smith, one of the directors, read 'an able, eloquent and satisfactory statement'.[2] The directors were 'fully and honourably acquitted of all the Complaints lately preferred against them, and are entitled to our warmest thanks, for the assiduity, diligence and integrity with which they have managed the affairs of the Company'.

Trade continued to decline; by 1816 it was reported that the trade to Dublin was reduced by one-third and that the traffic from the city had nearly ceased. The traders appealed for reductions in their rents for stores and this was granted. Tolls were reduced to 2d (Ir) per ton per mile and the traders agreed to make a corresponding reduction in freights. Nicholas Fanning, the chairman in 1816, went to London to discuss the financial difficulties with the government. The company had no funds to produce the one-third required to claim the final instalment of the 1812 grant. A letter marked 'Private and Confidential' was sent to Fanning in London in which he was told that a loan of £10,000 (Ir) would not be sufficient to extricate the company, £7,000 (Ir) was owed to the fund for discharging the debt, £20,000 (Ir) had been borrowed from two directors, there was no cash in hand to meet the present commitments and the revenues of the company were still falling. Another letter advised Fanning that 'none but the most decisive measure can rescue the Company from impending ruin'.

A new loan of £15,000 (Ir) was raised, but despite this in October 1816 the directors had to admit to the loanholders that there were no funds to meet the half-yearly payments on the loan debentures: 'If it be asked at what period it is likely we shall be able to resume the payment of any portion of the Interest,' they added, 'We have only to state that with the information now laid before you, you will be equally competent with us to form a judgement.' The loanholders recommended further retrenchments; they suggested that the directors' salaries should be suspended, all the stores should be let even at reduced rents and efforts should be made to sell all the coal on bank at the collieries. They asked for a clear statement of the company's finances at the next meeting unobscured by 'conjectural matter'.

Many people must have been badly hit by the suspension of the annual dividend and the decline in the value of canal stock. One shareholder, William Blair, applied for the position of lock-keeper on the Circular Line, 'as I have vested my property in Canal Stock, and from which I have not for some considerable time derived any Emolument, it has become imperative on me to endeavour to discharge the duties of this humble and laborious appointment'. The directors replied that they were 'deeply affected' by his application, no person of his rank in life had ever held such a position. He was appointed to the 3rd lock on the Circular Line, responsible for the first three locks, at the normal wage of 9s (Ir) per week and, in response to numerous appeals, he eventually received an increase of 1s 6d (Ir). He remained the lock-keeper until his death in 1837 when his grandson succeeded him.

In January 1817 the plundering of boats recommenced. Robert Whitton, the collector at Sallins, reported that 150 bags of flour were taken by an armed mob of about 200 men. Three of the directors went to investigate and reported that the people were instigated 'more from the desire of Plunder than from want'. The stolen flour was carried away for sale not only in Dublin but in various parts of the country, 'and after the spoil was divided among the first plunderers, the weaker were in their turn robbed by the Stronger'. The government was very slow to strengthen the military forces along the canal. William Evans appealed for immediate reinforcements at Rathangan and George Cross, an overseer, reported that 'the people of Prosperous near Robertstown, driven to desperation, declare themselves to be regardless of the Consequences of their Conduct'. The bankruptcy of Robert Brooke's cotton mills at Prosperous in 1786 had thrown more than half the people out of work and the condition of the people in the area had steadily deteriorated.[3]

Andrew Bagot, investigating the plunder of two more boats near Rathangan, said that there were not sufficient military in the vicinity to prosecute a search although there were traces of oatmeal in the streets and in some of the houses. He recommended that in future the trade boats should move in groups with strong military escorts, but while this was being organised, the list of plunders grew.

There are some interesting references to the plundering of boats in this area in the minute books of a parish near Rathangan.[4] In 1817 money was raised to help members of the parish who were being threatened by the law for their alleged part in the plunder, 'altho' said sum is now granted yet the raising of the same is to be suspended till such Time as its application as above may become necessary, when a special meeting of the Parish is to be called to judge of its Propriety'. Money had to be raised to reimburse the people whose property had been plundered, in one case Messrs Berry, and this money was later raised off the county at large and refunded to the parishioners.

The canal was breached maliciously in several places and John Stokes, reporting from one of the breaches, said that when it was nearly repaired, the men at work were surrounded by a large crowd: 'the imposing manner and appearance of these people is so bold and so ripe for Villany, that the efforts of a few Individuals without military aid, are of little service'.

Some arrests were made and fourteen of the plunderers were tried at Naas. The judge, stressing the leniency of the Grand Canal Company in not making capital prosecutions, committed the prisoners to jail until the next assize when he said he would pass sentences of transportation for life if the outrages continued. This threat, coupled with an increase in military strength and the introduction of convoys, halted the outrages. One more boat was plundered and a report said: 'It was melancholy to hear the cries of the unfortunate men under sentence of transportation. I understand their Friends are using all the exertions in their power to apprehend the persons concerned in the plunder.' By the close of 1817 most of the military reinforcements had been withdrawn.

With order restored on the canal, the directors turned their attention to the financial problems of the company. The troubled state of the country and the partial failure of the potato crop in 1817 had caused an even sharper decline in trade. It was impossible to carry out further retrenchments. A saving of £8,246 (Ir) per year had been achieved since 1810 but it was felt that if the salaries were reduced yet again it would not be possible to find 'Men of Integrity and Competent Talents' to discharge the duties. The directors were forced to use some of the sinking fund to meet the payments of interest on the debentures and this action was questioned by some of the shareholders. Eventually the loanholders agreed to accept a reduced rate of interest and this enabled the board to raise enough money to claim the last instalment of the 1812 grant towards the liquidation of the debt. In 1818 the government was informed that the debt had been reduced from £1,167,750 (Ir) to £954,250 (Ir), but the large figure remaining offered a bleak outlook for the company.

Daniel Bagot, the secretary, died in 1817 and was succeeded by Edward Lawson, who played an increasingly active part in the company's affairs until he retired in 1836. Because of a disagreement with the Rev Pomeroy, the owner of the Dawson

Street premises, the company moved to 50 William Street in 1818. This was the administrative centre of the company until 1863 when it was decided to centralise all the administration at James's Street Harbour.

In 1820 the situation was still deteriorating and the directors reported to the shareholders:

> The stoppage of the Distilleries, the slackness of Demand for Corn and above all the general stagnation of Foreign and Domestic Trade throughout the whole United Kingdom have concurred with one of the longest frosts that ever intercepted your navigations to produce an extraordinary deficiency in your Trade and Passage Boats, and reduce your revenues considerably below the average amount.

In the same year trouble flared up among the turf* traders. It had always been a difficult trade to control. Before the construction of the Circular Line the turf had been brought to James's Street where it was sold and dispatched around the city. In 1792 a mob, armed with blunderbusses and swords, attacked the boats at the harbour and demanded a reduction in the price of turf. The company ordered that each boat must carry a board setting out the price of the turf, at that time about 1s 5d (Ir) per kish or basket. When the Circular Line was completed, the traders used quays at various places to dispose of their turf and an inspector of turf boats was appointed to try to control the rapidly expanding trade. By 1808, 33,000 tons were arriving in the city each year and the company allowed a fixed toll of £6 (Ir) per boatload to encourage more traders.

By 1820, therefore, a considerable trade had been established and over ninety boats were engaged in the carriage of turf. The boats varied a great deal in size, though the fixed toll encouraged some traders to build larger boats. Originally the turf was sold direct from the boats but, in order to achieve a quicker turn around and avoid the boats occupying quay space, the company offered a bounty of 10d (Ir) per ton to traders who stored the turf in yards. Both these factors operated against the small

* In Ireland peat fuel is called turf.

OPENING of the NEW DOCKS in St GEORGES DAY 1796.

Page 87   Dublin: (*above*) the opening of the docks at Ringsend, 23 April 1796;
(*below*) Huband Bridge on the Circular Line

Page 88 Canal furniture: (*above*) ropemarks on Ballymanus Bridge near Athy; (*centre*) a mooring post at Lowtown, 1960; (*below*) a milestone on the long level marked in Irish miles

Lots for cutting Turf, in the
Bog of Knockballiboy.

TO BE LET,

THE several Lots of Bog, marked No. 1, to No. 31, in the Grand Canal Company's Bog near Philipstown.

Proposals to be received by the Company's Land Agent, Benjamin Booker, Esq. or by Mr. Kennedy, Collector at Philipstown; in whose Hands a Map of the Premises may be inspected.

By Order,

DANIEL BAGOT.

21st April, 1813.

FIGURE 11. Turf lots to be sold

trader and this, together with the low prices of the recession period, threatened the livelihood of many of them. They were driven to committing acts of violence against the larger traders. Boats were attacked by armed mobs and burnt or sunk. The swing beams of the 18th lock were cut off and a notice affixed:

> Take notice—that we do not wish to use any violence without noticing you of it and if you do not put a Stop to Yarding Turf which is the cause of all our distress we the aggrieved Bogmen does not wish to injure the Hon-Board or Trade But if the yards be not cut off remember Locks, Bridges and Aqueducts will be destroyed and a total finish put to the Trade. Forward this to the Grand Canal Company immediately. On account of Yarding Turf we paid a visit to the 18th lock on Friday night April 28th 1820.

A meeting was arranged in the hotel at Robertstown and the small traders were promised by a deputation from the board that the number of turf berths, where they would be allowed to clamp their turf to await sale, would be increased. This

F

relieved the situation, but rivalry between the traders continued and trouble occurred from time to time.

Distress in the country was increasing and several breaches were made maliciously on the Gallen level in an effort to obtain employment. On one occasion a crowd of 300 assembled and held up the repair work by throwing stones until the number of workers was increased considerably. In the end the company had to import labour from other areas in an attempt to stop these breaches in this district.

In 1822 Lord Downshire, writing to the board in connection with repairs to the Blundell aqueduct, said that the country around Edenderry was quiet, 'but the district is very ill off as many others are for active Magistrates which I fear is likely to continue as long as Capital and residence are withdrawn from the Country'. Later that year the partial failure of the potato crop brought about increasing distress and the company allowed a remission of tolls on cargoes of potatoes going to the west of Ireland to relieve distress. A few boats were attacked but the company tightened security and prevented a recurrence of the earlier outbreaks of violence. In November John Forrest, the collector at Lowtown, reported that he had been visited by a large party of armed men looking for firearms and he was asked if he 'had heard of the Prophecy which would soon be fulfilled of all the Protestants being swept away, and that the time is now very near when it would be so'.

Improved roads had brought about increasing opposition from land carriage and the board was forced to make further reductions in tolls to enable the traders to reduce their freights. It will be shown in the next chapter that the passage boats suffered a similar period of opposition. The company felt that the best way to fight this competition was to extend the canal system and so decided to follow up some of the schemes which had been considered in earlier years.

An extension of the navigation to Ballinasloe had been suggested even before the main line had reached the Shannon. A scheme to make the River Suck navigable had been laid before the government committee in 1800 and between 1802 and 1807 the Grand Canal Company made repeated efforts to persuade the directors-general to finance a similar scheme.[5] At this time the company was carrying out restoration work on the middle Shannon and it was pointed out that the work could be undertaken at a greatly reduced cost while the men and materials were on hand. Killaly estimated that it would cost £26,460 (Ir) with trackways or £15,781 (Ir) without, but the scheme was not authorised and the matter was dropped.

In 1817 the government had established the Exchequer Loan Commissioners in an attempt to try to relieve distress and poverty. The commissioners were empowered to finance schemes to provide employment and improve the country's economy. The canal company, therefore, decided to apply for a loan to construct a canal to Ballinasloe. It was decided to put forward a plan for a canal instead of using the River Suck. The canal would be a continuation of the existing Grand Canal from Shannon Harbour and would save the heavy expenditure involved in constructing trackways not only along the Suck but up the several miles of river to the confluence of the two rivers. It is interesting that this decision was made just before the arrival of steam boats on the Shannon; these would have rendered the construction of towpaths unnecessary and made the less costly river scheme more practical.

The company asked for a loan of £46,413 (Ir) and pointed out that the tolls from the canal would be used to pay off the loan. The scheme was turned down because the commissioners felt that the tolls were not sufficient security, but the company continued to press its application and, finally, in 1822, the loan was made available. John Killaly, now engineer to the directors-general, suggested that he would act as consultant engineer if his son, Hamilton, were allowed to superintend the work. Hamilton had joined the canal company the previous year as superintendent of the Shannon Line and the board agreed to this proposal and promoted him to superintend the new canal.

Tenders were received from Messrs Henry, Mullins &

HARTON'S

GRAND CANAL COACH,

Carrying Six Infide and Two Outfide Paffengers,.

SETS out from CLONONY-BRIDGE, every Morning, at Nine o'Clock, arrives in BALLINASLOE at half paft Eleven—Returns from BALLI NASLOE at Four o'Clock in the Evening, and arrives in SHANNON. HARBOUR at half paft Six.

Infide Paffengers - - -. • - 5s. 5d. Each.

Outfide Paffengers - - - • • 3s. 3d. Do.

Seats to Ballinafloe to be taken of the Mafters of the Paffage Boats.

Printer—D. DALY—Athlone.

FIGURE 12. Harton's coach connects with the passage-boats before the Ballinasloe branch is built

McMahon and Messrs Bergin, McKenna and Wood. The latter's estimate to complete the canal in 3 years for £40,000 (Ir) was accepted but shortly after this the canal company withdrew the contract because of a dispute about levels. Henry, Mullins & McMahon then agreed to complete the canal in 3½ years for £40,500 (Ir) but again the contract nearly broke down because of the difficulty of determining the levels of the canal in advance. Eventually a compromise was reached; any alteration in the levels shown in the surveys would have to be authorised by Killaly senior.

The company had already commenced drainage operations. In 1824 the contractors took over and soon over 1,000 men were at work. There was great distress among the people in this area and the work was very welcome. Bernard and M. B. Mullins in their paper already referred to in Chapter 2 gave a very good description of the methods they used to construct this canal. It was 14½ miles long, twelve of which were through bogland, with two rising locks, one at the junction with the Shannon and the other at Kylemore. The depth of bog averaged from 26ft to 46ft and they worked out a plan based on their earlier experience. This time they dug a channel along the centre line of the canal with channels on either side which would eventually form the outer edge of the canal. Similar drains were opened at 4 and 10 perches from the centre crossed by transverse drains. This produced a uniform subsidence over a wide area and avoided the necessity of high embankments. The contractors claimed that two-fifths of the cost could have been saved if they had been allowed to take five years to complete the canal.

In the summer of 1825 John Killaly reported that the work was proceeding well, 'a new and judicious system pursued with respect to the mode of drainage having confined the subsidence in a great measure to the line of the Canal, leaving the sides hard and compacted'. He said that he had authorised a 3ft alteration in the level between the two locks and this was immediately challenged by the directors who asked why they had not been consulted. Killaly reminded them that it had been agreed that these decisions should rest with him and said that he was very hurt by the tone of their letter. 'I must beg leave respectfully', he added, 'to decline interfering any further in the management of their concerns.' The board apologised and he withdrew his resignation.

In May 1826 Hamilton Killaly was able to report that the canal should be finished by early next year and the board agreed to his father's suggestion that he should be transferred to supervise the new extension to Mountmellick, which had been authorised by the loan commissioners. However, it was not until August 1827 that the completed canal was inspected by Mr Halpin, an engineer acting for the loan commissioners. He reported that he had found a number of discrepancies in comparison with the contract specifications and this brought another outburst from John Killaly. He said he was astonished that anyone 'conversant with the Science of Civil Engineering', viewing this 'stupendous undertaking . . . would not in his admiration of what has under the circumstances in so short a space of time been accomplished thro' so great an extent of an almost impassable morass, lose all recollections of petty deficiencies'. He added that it was impossible to execute works on such a large scale 'with mathematical accuracy of precision' and he quoted the example of Clonfert Bridge which, because of the lack of solid foundation, had to be built on piles instead of the specified solid foundation, which had been found to be 32ft below the surface of the bog.

Following the inspection, the canal was filled with water and the contractors were reminded that their contract would expire in November. They claimed that the board had delayed them by refusing to allow the canal to be filled until it was inspected and said that the canal would be ready in June of the following year. A small breach held up the opening for a few weeks but Killaly, who had been asked to carry out a very thorough inspection because of the suggestion that the canal was not up to specification, then reported that the works 'present throughout an appearance of perfection and stability equal to, if not surpassing those of any other Canal I am acquainted with'. The directors inspected the canal in the presence of Killaly and the contractors, and it was opened to traffic on 29 September 1828.

In the first year trade was good and the company handed over the net profit of £790 to the commissioners. The final amount lent had been £43,485 with an additional £2,769 for a wooden bridge across the Shannon. This bridge, which was fitted with an opening span near the east bank of the river, enabled the boats to be towed across to the new canal. The crossing point was wide and exposed and it must have been quite a dangerous operation in stormy weather; sometimes for their own safety the passengers were advised to make the crossing on foot. It had become very unsafe by the 1840s and the Shannon commissioners replaced it with a ferry in 1849.

Because of the nature of the terrain the canal was very vulnerable to malicious attacks and numerous small breaches were made in the 1830s, usually by people living in the area who hoped to be employed in the repair work. In 1831 John Stokes reported that the general condition of the canal was not good: some of the banks had been shaken by the breaches and heavy swells were rising in the bottom, limiting the depth considerably. Then in October 1832 a serious breach occurred, and so much of the bank was swept away that it was impossible to say whether it had been caused maliciously. One embankment had been swept away and the other one had rolled over into the canal. Crowds assembled demanding work and a military guard had to be provided to protect the company's officers. Eighty perches had to be remade, and in December Stokes reported that the work was proceeding slowly:

> The state of the Country here I fear is alarming, the People are decidedly the Governing party—their Law is enforced by a threat of Blood, and no one is willing to contend it with them . . . the nearer we approach to a finish, the greater the delay to every movement . . . Mr Seery and your humble servant in a great measure shut up in this abominable and dangerous quarter, that I am really at a loss what to do.

The repairs took over three months and the canal was reopened early in February.

One year later, in 1834, another serious breach occurred. This time the company had evidence that it had been caused maliciously because the spade marks were clearly visible; 50ft of bank had been carried away and the repairs took several months. Attempts had been made on several occasions to claim malicious injuries from the county but the Galway juries were not sympathetic and, even when a claim was allowed, the damages were reduced to a nominal figure.

In August 1835 the tunnel under the canal at Clonfert collapsed. It was repaired and collapsed again and it became obvious that more extensive repairs would have to be undertaken. Stokes reported that the wood used by the original contractors had been of very poor quality and a letter was sent to them informing them of this report involving 'their high professional character'. This letter evoked little response, though they reminded the canal company that they had offered to maintain the canal for ten years for £30 per Irish mile, but their offer had been rejected. The repairs took three months and the company had to pay a drawback of 2s (10p) per ton to the traders from Ballinasloe to encourage them to transport their goods by road to Shannon Harbour while the repairs were in progress.

Trouble continued and in 1838 Stokes recommended that no local labour should be employed as these tactics had worked well on the Shannon Line. He submitted a report pointing out the difficulty of protecting this canal where a few men could so easily cause considerable damage, and suggesting that the banks should be piled to prevent whole sections being swept away. When yet another breach was reported in November 1839, a deputation of directors inspected the damage and Stokes was authorised to use piles to strengthen the banks. The canal was reopened by the end of December but by May a new breach had occurred. This time Stokes blamed the original contractors again because the canal had caved in where it crossed an old river bed. These were hard years in the west of Ireland and Stokes said that he had been able to cut the wages from 1s (5p) to 10d (4p) per day, 'which has been at once acceded to without complaint'.

The piling achieved results because, thereafter, except for some minor trouble, the canal remained secure. Bernard and M. B. Mullins in their 1846 paper had said that it was a mistake to drive piles in a bog embankment 'as they disunite the particles, and open a way for the water to escape, thus increasing the evil they were intended to remedy'. In the light of all that had happened it is hard to understand how they could refer to the Ballinasloe Canal as 'the most recently and, we may be permitted to say, skillfully executed, from experience previously acquired'. By the 1840s over 14,000 tons of goods were being carried annually on the canal and the passage boats were catering for a large number of passengers in conjunction with coaching establishments at Ballinasloe, but the maintenance

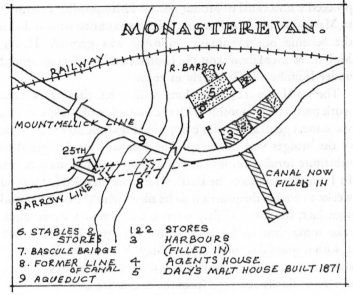

FIGURE 13

costs of the canal were so high that there was seldom any profit to hand over to the loan commissioners.

The Mountmellick Line had also been under consideration for many years before it was constructed. The Queen's County Canal Company, formed in 1800, planned to construct a canal from Monasterevan to Castlecomer via Mountmellick and Portlaoise (Maryborough). Surveys were made by John Killaly and Mitchell Sparks. Killaly, who surveyed the line from Monasterevan to Maryborough, said that he found no reason to deviate from an earlier survey by William Chapman, which had suggested the construction of an aqueduct over the Barrow at Monasterevan to replace the cumbersome system of locking down into the river and up again.[6] Some negotiations took place between this company and the Grand Canal Company but no active steps were taken to implement the scheme. Finally, in 1824, with the Ballinasloe Canal well in hand, the Grand Canal Company directors decided to seek a new loan to proceed with a canal to Mountmellick with a possible extension to Maryborough. The loan commissioners at first turned down the scheme but eventually approval was granted. Henry, Mullins & McMahon won the contract and work commenced under Hamilton Killaly early in 1827.

The canal was 11½ miles long with three rising locks and work proceeded smoothly with the exception of a dispute with some local gentlemen who complained that the ascent to some of the bridges was too steep. The company finally agreed to substitute turning bridges at Portarlington and Monasterevan. In June 1829 trade on the Barrow Line was stopped for several weeks to enable the junction to be made with the new line and aqueduct, but John Killaly warned that the new canal might take some time to fill because the dry gravelly soil would absorb a great deal of water. In May of the following year it was still not staunch and it was not until March 1831 that the canal was finally accepted from the contractors.

Hamilton Killaly had resigned in May of the previous year to take up an appointment with the Ulster Canal Company and he subsequently emigrated to Canada in 1834, two years after his father's death. The supervision of the canal fell on John Stokes, who continued to report difficulty in keeping the level up to even 3ft after it was opened to traffic. A lengthy dispute with the Rev Mr Kemmis about one of the water supplies did not help and in the 1830s the canal suffered a number of small malicious breaches which involved the company in a large number of claims from adjoining landowners for damage to their properties. Trade built up slowly; in the years 1831-4 the total revenue from the canal amounted to £1,429 and the net profit of £342 was handed over to the loan commissioners. In succeeding years the profit never exceeded £100; the original loan had amounted to £33,416.

The suggestion of a canal to Kilbeggan had been explored in 1796. The Grand Canal Company had been approached by a group of local gentlemen but, although the directors assured them of 'reasonable encouragement and assistance', they said that they did not feel justified in undertaking the construction of the canal at that time. Gustavus Lambert raised the subject again in 1806, saying that it was proposed to construct a narrow canal. The Grand Canal directors said they would be prepared to pay the difference in cost to enable a canal to be built which would conform with the existing line. The project was not pursued and in 1827, encouraged by its success in obtaining the other loans, the Grand Canal board decided to apply for a new loan to finance a canal to Kilbeggan. The loan was approved but the Royal Canal Company lodged an objection saying that the branch would interfere with its trade and loan approval was withdrawn. Finally, after a great deal of negotiation, the loan was again authorised in December 1828.

The company accepted a tender from William Dargan, who undertook to complete the canal in one year for £12,850 and work began in the summer of 1830. William Dargan had just taken over the contract to complete the Ulster Canal from Henry, Mullins & McMahon, who had withdrawn following a dispute with Thomas Telford.[7] Dargan was to become one of Ireland's foremost railway contractors and played an active part in setting up transport companies. This undertaking in the field of canal construction was not to prove a very happy one and he must have subsequently regretted his involvement in it.

The canal was 8 miles long with no locks and relied for its water supply on back water from the main line. John Stokes viewed the work in the course of the first year and criticised the methods being used in constructing the embankment and aqueduct over the Silver River, which he felt would not prove staunch. The directors paid very little attention to his warning and said that it was the business of the contractor to provide 'a perfectly staunch navigable canal'. By August 1831 Dargan reported that the canal had almost been completed except for the harbour which had not been included in the original contract. It was not, however, until the end of the next year that the water was let into the canal, whereupon the Silver River embankment leaked so badly that Dargan had to reline it with more clay.

In December of that year, 1832, an advertisement appeared in the press, purporting to come from the canal company, seeking proposals from competent persons 'to finish the canal'. The directors assured Dargan that it was a 'malicious forgery', but relations were not improving. Dargan insisted that he had built the Silver River embankment to Killaly's specifications and undertook to strengthen it for 'a fair and moderate remuneration'. 'I have now many strong reasons', he added, 'for wishing to get this work expeditiously out of hands.' His contracts with the Ulster Canal Company and the Dublin & Kingstown Railway Company were demanding all his attention.

Throughout 1833 Dargan continued his efforts to staunch the embankment without success. A deputation of directors visited the canal and found that it was 'very defective in depth, trackways and staunchness, and other respects' and Dargan was told that the company would not accept the canal in such a condition. In March 1834 Dargan was reminded that the date for the completion of his contract had been May 1831 and legal proceedings would be taken against him if it was not ready by April. He continued to try to staunch the canal and, finally, the board agreed to accept the canal if Dargan undertook to remedy all defects which might arise for the next six months. Dargan agreed to this and the canal was opened to traffic on 1 January 1835.

Dargan now asked for an additional £5,000 and after a great deal of correspondence the board agreed to pay him £1,000. Trade boats were finding it difficult to pass through the canal and in July, in the presence of Dargan, a boat drawing 4ft 6in was brought through to Kilbeggan. It took all day with a team of four horses and ten men, so Dargan had to carry out some further work. In August he wrote demanding the £4,000 which he claimed the company still owed him and he issued a writ for payment. The board replied with a writ against him for breach of contract. Finally, he agreed to accept £2,657 'in full of all demands on account of the Kilbeggan Canal, I beg that it may be understood that from and after Monday next, I shall be relieved from any other expence for maintenance or care of said Canal', and on 1 February 1836 the canal was taken off his hands. It gave very little trouble in the years that followed; a tunnel under the canal collapsed in 1840 and there were a number of malicious breaches in 1849. There was not a great deal of trade and the canal rarely made a net profit of more than £100 to hand over towards the repayment of the loan, which had amounted to £14,000.

The three canals, Ballinasloe, Mountmellick and Kilbeggan, became the subject of a complicated deal with the government in 1844. The canals were handed over to the canal company and the loans (including interest) still outstanding, amounting to £98,524, were commuted to £10,000. It will be shown later that this deal was the result of lengthy negotiations with the government about compensation for work carried out on the middle Shannon.

By 1825 the company's debt stood at £867,700 (Ir), on which the annual interest was £30,994 (Ir), half the interest paid in 1813. After 1 January 1826 Irish currency was replaced by British currency and, thereafter, all transactions were carried out in the new currency, new loan debentures being issued to equalise the different descriptions of debentures.

In 1836, with revenues rising in all departments, the company paid a dividend of 1 per cent. This angered Richard Corballis, one of the directors, and Charles Hopes, a loan-holder. They claimed that the company had promised to repay the 1814 debentures as soon as funds became available and they took the company to court on the issue. The case was dismissed, but the board agreed to pay £100 each for their £100 debentures. In 1838 Dr Henry Fulton, another shareholder, issued a strong condemnation of the manner in which the company's affairs were being conducted.[8] Amongst other things he accused the board of 'suffering the accounts and books of the

Company generally to be kept in such a state of mistifycation, confusion and irregularity, that it is impossible for any Director or Proprietor to comprehend them'.

Trade had gradually improved since the depressing times of the 1820s. In 1822 134,939 tons had been carried on the canal, the lowest figure for many years, but by 1837 the tonnage had risen to 215,911. A breakdown of the tonnage between 1822 and 1837 is contained in the second report of the Railway Commissioners in 1838.[9] Agricultural products continued to be the principal commodities carried, with a steady trade in building materials, turf, coal, coke and culm and an increasing traffic in general cargo. In dry seasons this increase in trade caused a water shortage on some levels and in 1838 side ponds were constructed at the 20th lock (Ticknevin) and subsequently at the 16th and 17th locks.

In December 1839 John Macneill, who was soon to become a prominent railway engineer,[10] was asked to carry out a survey of the canal. He continued to act as consultant engineer to the company and, when John Stokes died in 1843, he agreed with the board that it would not be necessary to appoint an engineer to succeed Stokes. In the following year, however, he resigned from his commitment to the canal company to become engineer to the Great Southern & Western Railway Company. He was knighted in the same year at the opening of the Dublin & Drogheda railway. The board of the canal company decided to print his final report on the state of the canal.[11]

The position of the company was improving but a new and much more dangerous threat to its prosperity was soon to be revealed with the coming of the railways.

CHAPTER 5

The Passage Boats

BEFORE continuing the story of the company into the 1840s, this is a convenient point to return to a consideration of the passage boats. It will be remembered that a passage boat had begun to ply as soon as the canal was completed to Sallins and the service was extended to Robertstown in 1784. John Wesley was a passenger in this boat in the following year:

> Wednesday 22nd June 1785. I went, with twelve or fourteen of our friends, on the canal to Prosperous. It is a most elegant way of travelling little inferior to that of Trackskuyts in Holland. We had fifty or sixty persons in the boat, many of whom desired me to give them a sermon. I did so, and they were all attention.[1]

By 1790 there were six boats operating and the directors appointed a superintendent of passage boats, H. Cowell, to control the expanding business. It had been reported that 'spirits are now sold and other Irregularities committed' on board the boats and one of the masters was fined £5 (Ir) for allowing wine to be taken 'to such excess as to have incommoded a Lady on Board in so great a Degree as probably to prevent Her or any other Female passing on the Boats in future'.

The newspapers provide occasional reports of incidents on the boats. Two young men, found cheating at cards, 'were not only obliged to refund the cash they had unjustly pocketed, but narrowly escaped being severely ducked by their fellow passengers'.[2] On 2 July 1791 the directors were enraged by a report in the *Freeman's Journal* which they said was greatly exaggerated:

> Sunday last, a very unlucky accident happened on the Grand Canal. As one packet boat was coming in and another going out —the driver belonging to one of them neglected to slacken the rope, to let the other pass, by which it skimmed along the gunnel, and swept off all before it—the passengers who were on the deck, baggage and all. Some were thrown into the Canal, and others dashed into the adjoining boat, severely hurted and bruised. . . . This it seems was owing to the impudence of the drivers—an ignorant stiffness, not to give way to each other, waiting to see which would slacken his rope first. The Conductors of these packet boats should punish such ruffianly obstinacy—as it is dangerous to the lives of the passengers.

In December 1792, just before Christmas, a more serious accident occurred in which eleven people perished. This was the only occasion in the history of the company's passage boats when an accident resulted in loss of life, although there were occasions when individual passengers fell from the boats and were drowned:

> Yesterday morning, a melancholy consequence of the drunkenness usual at this season of the year occurred on the Grand Canal. Upwards of one hundred and fifty people, many of them intoxicated, forced themselves in spite of repeated remonstrances from the Captain, in on the early Athy passage boat. He often, in vain, told them the boat was overloaded, and must sink if many of them did not withdraw; at length, from their numbers and turbulence the boat was overset, near the 8th lock, and five men, four women and two children perished— the rest of the passengers escaped. . . . We are happy to learn, that the principal cabin passengers were timely alarmed by the conduct of the unfortunate rioters and drunken people, and all left the boat at the different locks, so that no person of any note, save the Captain (White) has suffered.[3]

Captain White was master of the *Huband* passage boat at this time so this must have been the boat involved in the accident. Four of the victims were from one family, a father, his daughter and her two children; the girl was returning to her husband in the country and her father was accompanying her for part of the journey.[4]

The service had been extended to Athy by 1791. The boats left Dublin at 5am and reached Athy at 6pm. In May 1797 a service to Philipstown (Daingean) commenced but it was interrupted shortly afterwards by the breach near the Blundell aqueduct. The fares at this time were 1s 1d (Ir) first cabin and 9d (Ir) back cabin per stage of about 8 miles. These charges did not compare favourably with the rates in the rest of Europe; DeLatocnaye said that they were nearly double the fare in Holland.[5] A report in the *Volunteers' Journal* in 1786 criticised the high charges, 'The fare . . . is dearer than on any inland navigation in Europe, and far exceeds the proportionate rates of land carriage'.[6]

There were at least eight boats in operation by 1797. They were usually named after directors or their wives and sometimes they were given the name of the lord lieutenant of the time. It is difficult to trace the history of individual boats because they were sometimes renamed to honour a particular person.

When the service was extended to Tullamore in 1798, a new scale of charges (Ir) was drawn up which showed a small increase:

Dublin to	State Cabin		Common Cabin		Distance Miles
	s	d	s	d	
Robertstown	4	10½	2	6	25
Philipstown (Daingean)	9	2½	5	1½	48
Tullamore	10	10	5	11½	56½
Monasterevan	7	7	4	0	40½
Athy	8	1½	4	8	54¼

The fare to Shannon Harbour (78½ miles), when the canal was finally opened, was 16s 3d (Ir) state cabin and 9s 5½d (Ir) common cabin. An occasional service was operated between Robertstown and Milltown in the early 1800s to facilitate encampments on the Curragh which were set up during the

G

GRAND CANAL.

Passage-Boat Horses.

THE Court of Directors of the GRAND CANAL COMPANY are ready to receive Proposals, for supplying able HORSES to draw the Company's PASSAGE-BOATS, to and from the following Stages, for three Years, to commence from the Expiration of the present Contract, viz.

STAGES.	Expiration of present Contract.
Tullamore to Shannon Harbour.	1st *May,* 1812.

Proposals to be sealed, and indorsed, " *Proposals for Horses;*" and to be delivered at the Secretary's Office, No. 38, Dawson-street, Dublin, on or before Tuesday, the tenth Day of March, 1812, before one o'Clock in the Afternoon ; on which Day the several Proposals will be opened and taken into Consideration.

NOTE.—The Form of Proposal to be had from the Secretary.

19th *February,* 1812.

By Order,

DANIEL BAGOT, *Sec.*

DUBLIN: PRINTED BY WILLIAM PORTER, 72, GRAFTON-STREET,
Printer and Stationer to the Grand Canal Company.

FIGURE 14. Seeking tenders for a new horsing contract

Napoleonic war; the fare was 1s 8d (Ir) state or 10d (Ir) common cabin.

The number of horse contractors had gradually increased, each contractor undertaking a two- or three-year contract to draw the boats on a specified stage. Fines were exacted for unpunctuality and sometimes the contractors proved very inefficient. In 1800, for example, the Sallins to Robertstown stage was reported to be 'very ill performed, there being sometimes only one weak ill-fed horse employed in that service'. By

1801 the company was paying over £5,000 per annum to the contractors, although some of this was recouped in fines. Remission of fines was allowed in the case of strong contrary winds, ice more than 1in thick and sometimes in the case of extreme hardship such as an epidemic of a horse disease. The company tried the experiment of conducting the Sallins-Dublin stage for a few years but before long it was given to a contractor again. In 1813 the board ordered that a special livery should be worn by the riders, 'blue frock coat, scarlet waistcoat, leather breeches and boots or long pantaloons lined with black leather (like those worn by Artillery Drivers), a glazed hat, and great coat with deep collar and large cape'.

In 1807 rising prices forced the company to increase the fares considerably. Competition from coach services was, however, increasing all the time and care had to be taken to keep the boat fares at a competitive rate. The fare from Dublin to Monasterevan by coach was 14s 1d (Ir) inside or 9s 9d (Ir) outside and the canal fare, with the increase, amounted to 10s 10d (Ir) state cabin or 6s 8d (Ir) common cabin. The war of rates continued: in 1810 the company was forced to lower the fares again to win back passengers from the coaches, and a further decrease in 1816 brought fares back to the 1790 rates.

Extra boats plied at certain times of the year, at Christmas, Easter, Whitsuntide and for the law terms, Quaker meetings and the Ballinasloe Fair, forty occasions in all. There are some interesting references to travel by canal at this time in the Leadbeater papers.[7] Mary Shackleton had married William Leadbeater in 1791 and they lived in Ballitore, County Kildare. They used to travel by road from there to meet the passage boat at Sallins. William brought Mary to Dublin after their marriage and she wrote to a friend describing the journey, 'the rest of the company seemed composed of half-gentry, there was card playing. We got the Captain's little room to ourselves where we were very cozy and Mansergh sent us a comfortable dinner from the great table.' There are several references in the correspondence to the boats being very crowded and there is a

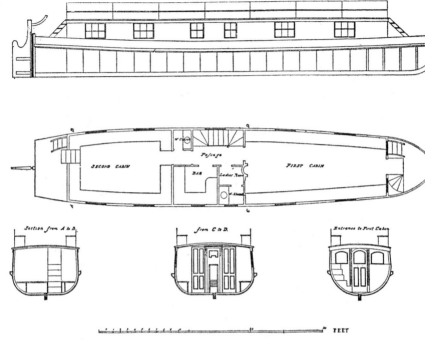

FIGURE 15. The layout of a passage-boat

long letter from a friend, Mary Mellor, describing how she fell in while disembarking from the boat and very nearly drowned. She was eventually rescued and brought to the Captain's house. She was loud in her praise of Captain Weekes and his wife, 'her care, cleverness and tenderness were far beyond what I could expect from a stranger'.

Captain Weekes had been one of the first passage boat masters. He and his wife were frequently reprimanded by the board for insolence and 'irregularities' of one sort or another. Eventually he was demoted from his position as senior boat master but was subsequently reinstated. Two years later he was again demoted and he appealed to the board:

Your memorialist and his wife have devoted themselves to the duties of their station for upwards of one and twenty years until at length they are grown grey in your service; Your memorialist hath often experienced your generous consideration for his involuntary faults. He now humbly prays your pardon for an error into which he has fallen not from contumnaciousness but by a misjudged zeal for your service contrary to the orders of his superior officer.

He was reinstated once again and, as will be seen in the next chapter, he was subsequently appointed hotelkeeper at Portobello, but he died before he could take up the position.

The crew consisted of a captain, steerer, stopman (whose job it was to check the boat's way entering the locks) and a boy or 'loose'. The master's wife and 'two suitable and decent girls' served the passengers. The captain's wages in the 1820s ranged from 1 to $1\frac{1}{2}$ guineas (Ir) per week depending on his seniority, the steerers received from 12s to 18s (Ir) and the stopmen 9s to 11s $4\frac{1}{2}$d (Ir). The boys did not receive any pay in these early days, but they were entitled to become stopmen after two years' service with one captain or in one boat.

The captains were frequently reprimanded and sometimes suspended for various offences such as card-playing with the passengers, using 'very indecent language and conduct in the presence of female passengers', breaking the company's regulations and drunkenness, the latter being by far the most common offence. The captain had the difficult task of keeping his passengers sober, in particular the people in the common cabin who were 'in the habit of intoxicating themselves by drinking excessive quantities of porter'. He had to see that the regulations were observed regarding the amount of alcohol allowed to passengers, who on no account were allowed to bring drink on board with them or 'visit houses' along the line.

In 1804 James Butler, Lord Dunboyne, was appointed 'Inspector of Passage Boats'. He was given apartments at Robertstown and received $1\frac{1}{2}$ per cent of the passage boat revenue. On one occasion he fell into the canal and one of the stopmen rescued him. The board decided to award the stopman four guineas (Ir), and it is amusing that the four was subsequently crossed out and a two inserted. Lord Dunboyne resigned for personal reasons in 1810 and Andrew Bagot, who was already inspector of trade, took on the additional post at a combined salary of £200 (Ir) per annum with an allowance of 5s (Ir) for each day spent west of Robertstown. After repeated requests his salary was increased to £300 and he continued to serve the company very actively until he was forced by ill health to retire in 1847. He was superannuated at £175 per annum and died three years later.

Henry Phillips, who was general manager of the company in the 1920s, made a detailed study of the company's history and built up a very good picture of the standard passage boat of this period.[8] The boats were 52ft by 9ft 10in, and the early ones cost as little as £202. There was accommodation for forty-five in the state cabin and thirty-five in the common cabin. There is an excellent description of the interior of one of these boats in an article entitled 'A Canal Boat Sketch' in *Duffy's Hibernian Magazine* in 1862. The author was travelling by train to Galway and thinking back to the days when she used to make the journey by canal:

> The cabin was a long, narrow apartment, along either side of which ran a bench covered with red moreen, and hard enough to have been stuffed with paving stones, but I believe it was really with chopped hay, and capable of accommodating on each seat fifteen uncrinolined individuals, who might sit there comfortably enough on a cold winter's day, with a roaring turf fire in the small grate, as I have done more than once, while the boat was being slowly forced through a sheet of ice, several inches in thickness. . . . Well, between the seats ran a narrow table of about a foot-and-a-half in width, which was now covered with the small parcels of the passengers—books, boxes, baskets, dressing cases, and oh, horror! a cage, containing a fine singing canary.

The back cabin had similar seats along either side but a third seat, on which the passengers sat back to back, occupied the place of the table. There were ventilators, but a crowded boat must have been very stuffy. Charles Lever and Anthony

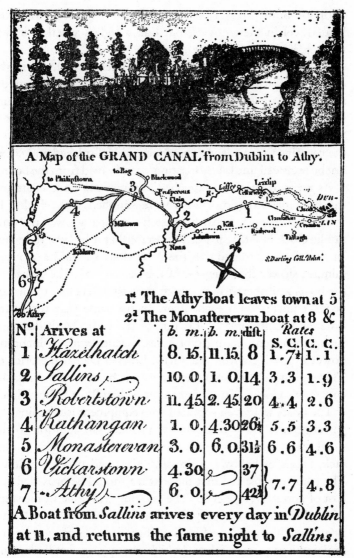

FIGURE 16. A passage-boat timetable

Trollope both drew from their practical experience of canal boat travel in their novels, but one wonders whether it was quite as bad as they suggested.[9]

Framed maps showing the canal routes were hung in the cabins and permission was given to people to hang up advertisements. Mrs McKenna, a schoolmistress from Rathangan, was allowed to display cards, detailing the terms of her school 'neatly framed and glazed'. Resolutions of censure passed on the captains for misdemeanours were also displayed and could not be removed until authorisation was received from the board.

As great attention was attached to punctuality, the boats and the principal stopping places were supplied with clocks. In 1798 it was reported that because the company's was the only public clock in Athy, it was important that it be kept in repair. In 1818 it was ordered that the Athy clock should be kept ten minutes slower than the rest of the line to make the arrival of the boats at Robertstown, where the passengers had to change boats, coincide with each other. In the same year the board ordered a 'chronometer' for one of the boats 'with detached Escapements and eight pivot holes jewelled with maintaining power expansive curbs and a hard Enamel Dial at the price of Thirty guineas'. For some reason it was the custom to keep the company's clocks two minutes slower than 'Post Office Time'.

The boats were well supplied with equipment for feeding the passengers. A 'List of Ordinary' included, in addition to the usual plates, glasses, linen and cutlery, six candlesticks, a toast rack, a pair of bellows, a dressing glass and two tea caddies. The company insisted that the best tea should be provided at a cost of about 8s (Ir) per lb. The cooking was done in the stern of the boat in two large pots on a small stove. In the 'Canal Boat Sketch', mentioned earlier, there is a description of the captain killing two chickens 'which were plunged still bleeding into the pot containing a leg of mutton'. This pot also contained carrots, parsnips, turnips and potatoes while the other pot contained bacon and cabbage. In 1818 the board ordered that as 'few live fowl as possible be suffered to be carried on

Board as considerable dirt and of a very offensive nature is created thereby'.

Trollope described the 'eternal half-boiled leg of mutton floating in a bloody sea of grease and gravy'.[10] Sir John Carr was less critical: 'We had an excellent dinner on board, consisting of a leg of boiled mutton, a turkey, ham, vegetables and porter and a pint of wine each at four shillings and ten pence a head.'[11] Sir John was writing in 1805 and the menu does not appear to have varied much over the years because in 1843 Herr Venedy travelled by boat to Ballinasloe and his description is very similar:

> The dinner was a solid meal. It consisted of bacon, legs of mutton, beef, potatoes and beer, and it was disposed of in such a manner as to shew that those who partook of it must have right good stomachs. After dinner, whiskey punch occupied the place of coffee.[12]

Prices seemed to vary a little depending on the state of the economy of the country but they remained essentially the same as these prices (Ir) for 1819:

	State Cabin		Common Cabin	
	s	d	s	d
breakfast with eggs	1	6	1	3
dinner	2	4	1	8
supper	1	6	1	1
pint of port or wine	2	6	not allowed	
porter		6		6
cider		10		10
naggin of spirits with sugar	1	1	not allowed	
tea or coffee after dinner	1	1	1	1
sugar after dinner		3		3

Children under ten paid half rates. No spirits were issued to women or children, and no smoking was allowed in either cabin.

The captains were obliged to buy their wines, spirits and porter from a merchant nominated by the board. I. B. Alloway, who was the company's pay-clerk for a number of years, supplied the boats from 1801–8 when, after several complaints that his wine and porter 'could not be drank being so infamously bad', the contract was won by Maurice Blake of Abbey Street, whose nephew, Martin D'Arcy, subsequently took over the contract and supplied the company until 1843. In that year the board authorised the captains to buy their supplies wherever they wished, because, although D'Arcy's whiskey was 'good and well flavoured, his wine was decidedly bad'.

It was the custom of the directors to proceed on an annual inspection of the line. These inspections lasted several days, the directors staying overnight in the company's hotels. It was always carefully minuted that the secretary should conduct the inspection with the greatest possible economy and £100 was voted to him, but this figure was reduced to £60 in later years. In 1803, in the course of an inspection, a board meeting was held on board the passage boat *Macartney* and a resolution was passed:

> The directors having for the sake of economy to the Company travelled in the Tullamore Passage Boat, and there being only two gentlemen passengers and no lady present resolved that the rule for limiting the wine to one pint per head only, be dispensed with for this day and no longer.

A number of guests were usually invited to join the annual inspection but this custom must have been abused, because in 1819 Mr Bagot was 'particularly desired to prevent the intrusion of all persons not included in the above order except such as the Board or the Committee shall specially desire the attendance of'. In later years an inspection was not held every year and, after the passage boats were withdrawn, although a boat was held in readiness for the directors, they did not visit the line very often.

The minute books contain many references to incidents of one sort or another on board the boats. In 1801 the lock-keeper of the 18th lock was given a guinea (Ir) for 'his care of the poor woman taken in labour in the boat'. On another occasion

Miss Sutton, a young lady passenger, was carried beyond her stopping place at the Blundell aqueduct, near Edenderry, and deposited 'at eleven o'clock of a dark night without any certainty of protection' at Colgan's Bridge. The captain was suspended and Colgan, who was supposed to keep the waiting-room open for the night boat, had his allowance withdrawn.

From an early time the company had encouraged and frequently subsidised coach operators who were prepared to run services to and from the boats. The earliest recorded example of this was Messrs Hayden & Lynch, who operated a coach in the 1780s which started from the city one hour after the boat and overtook it at the 11th lock; the same coach returned to the city with passengers who wished to avoid the last few miles of heavy lockage, the charge being 1s 7½d (Ir) per person. Most of the early coach proprietors do not appear to have stayed in business for very long and sometimes they proved a bad speculation for the canal company. In 1808 Major Ormsby was lent £1,000 (Ir) to set up a coaching establishment between Monasterevan and Cashel with a bounty of £60 (Ir) per year. Two years later he was declared a bankrupt and the company had the greatest difficulty in obtaining any money from his sureties.

In 1808 Luke Harton, who had taken a lease of the company's new hotel in Shannon Harbour, commenced a coach service from nearby Clononey Bridge to Ballinasloe (see page 92). The company agreed to pay him a 'deficiency payment' if his receipts did not exceed £600 (Ir) per year, and in some years this did not cost the company anything. The total fare from Dublin to Ballinasloe was £1 2s 9d (Ir) state cabin and inside on the coach or 14s 1d (Ir) common cabin and outside. Harton also started a service from Shannon Harbour to Birr in 1816; he charged 1s 3d (Ir) inside and 10d (Ir) outside and the company paid him a bounty of 2s 6d (Ir) for each state cabin passenger and 1s 6d (Ir) for each common cabin passenger. In 1818 the firm of W. H. Bourne began to run coaches in opposition from Clononey Bridge to Loughrea, Ballinasloe and

ATHLONE AND GILLAN
DILIGENCE,

Carrying THREE Infide and ONE Outfide PASSENGERS.

GEORGE FORREST

BEGS leave to acquaint his FRIENDS and the PUBLIC, that from and after the 13th of JANUARY, 1806, a Diligence will leave Gillan every Morning at the arrival of the Paffage Boat from Tullamore, and arrive in Athlone at Eleven o'Clock; and the fame Diligence will leave Athlone every Evening at One o'Clock, and arrive at Gillan before the arrival of the Paffage Boat from Shannon Harbour.

The above Diligence is eftablifhed principally for the accommodation of Ladies and Gentlemen who travel in the Grand Canal Paffage Boats, and the Fares are regulated accordingly, viz:

For every Infide Paffenger between Gillan and Athlone refpectively, who fhall alfo be a State Cabin Paffenger in the Boat, the whole way between Dublin and Gillan,   3s. 9dh.

For every other Infide Paffenger in the Diligence, between Gillan and Athlone refpectively,   4s. 10dh.

For every Outfide Paffenger that travels the whole way between Dublin and Gillan,   2s. 8dh.

For every other Outfide Paffenger between Gillan and Athlone,   3s. 3d.

Each Infide Paffenger is to be allowed 28lbs. of Luggage, free from Charge, and an Outfide Paffenger 10lbs.

All extra Luggage to be paid for before it is taken in, at the rate of One Penny per Pound.

Children on the Lap to pay half Infide Fare, and not prevent the full complement of Paffengers, otherwife to pay full Fare.

None allowed Outfide lefs than full Fare—no Places engaged, nor Paffengers or Parcels taken in, unlefs on payment of full Fare.

The Diligence to fet off precifely at the hour appointed, and all Paffengers not then attending, to forfeit their Fare.

The Proprietor will not be accountable for any Paffenger's Luggage.

Places to be taken for the Diligence, on Board the Paffage Boat from Dublin to Gillan.—Places to be taken for the Diligence, from Athlone to Gillan, at the Three Blacks, Athlone.

RATE of the FARE in the GRAND CANAL PASSAGE BOAT from GILLAN to DUBLIN.

STATE CABIN.

From Gillan to Tullamore,	-	-	-	2s. 8dh.
From Tullamore to Dublin,	-	-	-	15s. 2d.
Rates in the Diligence from Athlone to Gillan,		-		3s. 9dh.

Total Fare between Dublin and Athlone,   £ 1 1 8

The Driver to be paid 6dh. by each Infide Paffenger, and no more.

Printed by D. DALY, Athlone.

FIGURE 17. A diligence carries canal passengers to Athlone

Tuam. By this time Harton had fallen out with the canal company because he had raised his fares without consultation and, now, the company made a new agreement with Bourne which probably put Harton out of business.

The canal company had been glad of the opportunity to enter into an agreement with Bourne, because, as one of the larger firms, he had been one of a group who had appealed to the Lord Lieutenant to instruct the canal company to limit its activities to coach routes connecting with the canal. This arose because the canal company had been extending its influence and had sponsored a coach from Birr to Limerick. The company was warned that it must curtail these activities and in 1824 Bourne agreed to run a coach from Shannon Harbour to Limerick for a bounty of 2s (Ir) per passenger to or from the passage boat. The combined journey from Dublin to Limerick cost £1 11s (Ir) state cabin and inside the coach or 19s (Ir) common cabin and outside, but it was unable to compete with the direct coach route from Dublin and Bourne decided to withdraw the service after a few months.

Tullamore to Athlone was another route which the company tried to keep in operation. Andrew Morgan, the Tullamore hotelkeeper, agreed to run coaches on this route in 1817 and the company offered him a deficiency payment of £900 (Ir) per annum. The fare was 5s 5d (Ir) inside or 4s 2d (Ir) outside and, at first, he reported that it was a great success. He said that he was exceeding his guarantee and that 'several gentlemen who had travelled by the coach has declared to me that in England or Ireland They have never travelled in a better appointed coach'. Over 3,000 people used his coaches in 1818 but thereafter the numbers began to fall and the company reduced his guarantee to £750 (Ir). By 1829 Messrs Hartley & Desmond, an expanding coaching firm, were operating coaches direct from Dublin to Athlone and the canal company was forced to make reductions in fares.

Despite these reductions the number of passengers using the boats continued to fall and the directors were constantly exploring methods of increasing the boats' speed and efficiency. It is interesting to trace some of the inventions which were offered to the company for propelling boats prior to the introduction of the steam boat into Ireland. As early as 1782 Bartholomew Talbot said that he had invented a machine for propelling boats but, unfortunately, there are no details and nothing more was heard of Mr Talbot.

In 1807 Thomas Tunks of Hardwicke Street offered the company a machine 'by means of which two men may drive without horse, trackline or any other assistance from the land the Passage Boats at the same speed as before'. The directors did not show any interest in Mr Tunks but, one month later, Joseph Hardy said that 'by great study and perseverence' he had invented a machine to work the boats without horses. The company placed a boat at his disposal and supplied him with 'timber, iron and screw bolts' and he obtained 'metal wheels' in Belfast. His first two efforts were not a success and the board refused to allow him to continue; his machinery was dismantled and handed over to him.

It must be remembered that Symington's steamer, the *Charlotte Dundas*, had been tried out successfully in 1802 on the Forth & Clyde Canal, and these early years of the nineteenth century brought forward a great number of inventors.[13]

In 1809 John Maguire, one of the company's subscribers, asked for permission to try out his invention 'the Nautilus':

> In this machine, there are no complex movements, no Wheels, no Springs, its great power resting on the simplest of all the mechanical principles of force, namely that of the Lever, and may be increased to any degree of power, from that of a rowboat, to a ship of the line.

There is no record of any experiments with 'the Nautilus' and the directors were obviously becoming more cautious in their attitude to would-be inventors because in 1811 an application from Thomas Conroy was turned down: 'Several Plans of a similar nature having been from time to time laid before the Board, which were found not reducible to practice, they have

resolved not to interfere in the making of any further experiments but to wait until experience of others shall have proved
the usefulness and practicability of such a Plan'.

In 1814 James Dawson, one of the directors, designed and
patented his ideas for a steam boat.[14] The other directors had
viewed it in operation in the previous year, 'which being set in
motion appeared capable of going at the rate of near three miles
per hour, produced much less surge against the Banks of the
Canal than the Passage Boats drawn by horses, and, on the
whole, appears highly deserving of attention'. This boat was
double keeled and the wheel was mounted between the keels
in an effort to overcome the difficulty of operating conventional
paddle wheels in narrow locks. Although he was asked to
submit an estimate of the cost of his boat, the matter was not
pursued.

In the same year, 1814, Francis Sullivan offered a 'contrivence
. . . totally different from anything of the Kind I have hitherto
heard or read', in which, he said, he was supported by the
'favourable opinion of a Professor of Philosophy'. This was a
busy year for inventors; Samuel Downes submitted a model
which displayed a 'marked improvement in hydrostaticks',
and Louis LaFeuillade was granted the use of a boat to carry
out some experiments. He entered into a lengthy correspondence with the board about the financial arrangements he
would require when the company adopted his invention.
Daniel Finucane of Limerick was not so demanding; he was
prepared to supply his machine for 'ten guineas on being found
in materials. . . . I would ask no more than five guineas until
I would finish it to your satisfaction.' In 1816 Richard Maiben
entered into negotiations as to the terms he would require to
supply 'a better and less expensive mode of propelling boats
than has been hitherto adopted in this kingdom'. He suggested
£3,730 per annum, a figure based upon the saving which he
estimated his invention would effect.

By this time the paddle steamer *City of Cork*, launched by
Captain Christopher Owens in June 1815, was operating

successfully between Cork and Cobh.[15] The directors approached him for information and advice and also carried out some experiments in towing on the River Liffey with another steamer, the *Princess Charlotte*, when she visited Dublin in December 1816.

In 1822 James Scott, who had patented his invention 'of an accelerating lever-motion' two years earlier, was authorised to carry out some experiments at Ringsend basin, and the directors approached Goldsworthy Gurney in 1829 in connection with the application of his patented 'steam carriage' to drawing the passage boats.[16] At about this time a series of experiments was carried out with a boat designed by Mr Watson, manager of the Shannon Navigation Company, in which Charles Wye Williams and Robert Mallet were involved.[17] The boat was about 120ft long but it parted in the middle, the two parts joining together side by side to pass through locks. Mr Mallet was asked to design steam power for this boat and experiments proved that she could achieve speeds of 6 mph.

In 1831 William Houston introduced horse-drawn passage boats on the Glasgow, Paisley & Johnstone Canal which could travel at from 9 to 10mph. The boats were 70ft long and 5½ft wide and could accommodate seventy to eighty passengers. The hulls were of very light displacement formed of thin iron plates riveted together, and the cabin was made of wood covered with oiled cloth. Each boat was drawn by two horses, attached one behind the other, with the horse in front wearing 'blinders' and the rider on the second horse.[18] Scott Russell proved by experiments that, up to the speed of 7½mph, the resistance of the water increased as the square of the velocity of the boat, but at 8½mph the resistance decreased because the boat mounted on its own wave, instead of pushing it ahead, thereby diminishing the necessary traction.[19]

Some attempts had been made by the Grand Canal Company to produce a lighter iron passage boat. In 1828 William Mallet was asked to build one in the dock at Portobello. She was

Page 121 Canal hotels: (*above*) Robertstown in 1896, when the hotel was being used as a police barracks; (*below*) Portobello House in 1969, when it was a nursing home

Page 122 Canal hotels: (*above*) the junction to Tullamore Harbour with the hotel in the background, 1971; (*below*) Shannon Harbour canal boat rally, 1971, the hotel on the left

named the *Harty*, but she proved too heavy and was not a success even after modifications had been carried out. Iron boats were also built for the company by John Marshall, Courtney Clarke and Edward Murphy in the years that followed and, although they were lighter, they were still too heavy to attain high speeds. The remains of an iron passage boat lie submerged in the canal about two miles west of Daingean (Philipstown) which local tradition says is the *Hibernia*. She was one of the Irish boats built by Courtney Clarke in 1832 at the Ringsend Iron Works. Constructed of ⅛in thick sheet iron, she cost £275.

In October 1832 the board decided to send Andrew Bagot to Paisley to inspect the new fast boats and in the following year the first 'Scotch boat' was ordered from Mr Houston. The colourful 'fly boats'* were about to enter the Irish scene.

* Although these boats were sometimes referred to as 'swift boats' in the company's records, they soon became known as the 'fly boats', possibly because the fast-moving trade boat, traditionally called 'fly boat' in England, was not a feature of the Irish canals.

H

CHAPTER 6

The Fly Boats and the Hotels

ON 1 January 1834 the newly arrived 'Scotch Boat' was tried out for the first time. The directors were delighted with her performance and more boats were ordered at once. It was decided to set up a fast boat service by day and to continue to operate the night boats using the slower Irish iron boats. The fly boats commenced running on 1 May 1834. One left Portobello at 7am and arrived at Tullamore (58 miles away) at 4.05pm, and connecting boats reached Athy and the newly opened terminus of Mountmellick at 5pm. This timetable required an average speed of 6mph including locks. This performance was subsequently improved to an average of 8mph, which must have involved travelling at speeds considerably faster. The service to Shannon Harbour did not attract sufficient passengers and a boat to Kilbeggan was substituted, but with the rising tide of emigration, the Shannon Harbour fly boat was resumed in 1838 with an extension to Ballinasloe. The boats accommodated 20 state and 32 common cabin passengers; there were no cooking facilities but 'snacks of cold meat and a limited allowance of the usual liquors' were available.

The horse contractors did not find it easy to adhere to their contract times. One contractor, William Scully, said that 'certain ruin would be the consequence' if he were asked to keep to his time of 8 Irish mph. It appears that three or four horses were used which had to be frequently changed. One of the contractors, Henry Odlum, said that he needed 16 horses to operate his stage of 12 Irish miles. Some of the account books of another of the contractors, Robert Whyte, have survived and they provide an interesting insight into the horse-contracting business.[1] Robert had taken over the contract from his brother, Nicholas, who had failed to operate it efficiently and, as it will be seen, he also took over Nicholas's lease of the hotel at Robertstown when the latter died. Thus the account books have a twofold interest. Robert kept an income and expenditure account for one year from the commencement of the swift boats and showed that his profit was only £171. Hundreds of horses passed through his hands; many are listed with their names, date of purchase and price. In the 1830s he paid up to £16 for a good colt and as little as £5 for a horse with a blind eye.

Some of the contractors incurred heavy fines for loss of time and strict checks were kept if boats were slowed down by stress of weather. The canal was seldom closed by ice for more than a day or two at a time each winter and it was usually possible to keep it open by using specially strengthened ice boats. It is interesting that in all the years until the passage boats were withdrawn in 1852 there were less than twenty occasions when it was reported to the board that traffic had been interrupted by ice. Most of these were of short duration, although in the winter of 1813–14 the canal was closed for five weeks and there were lengthy stoppages in 1819–20, February 1838 and 1846–7. There is a vivid description of the canal in February 1838 in a report by John Stokes:

At the Wren's Nest Overfall on the Gollardstown level, found the Ice Boat completely deserted, her people having left her the night before—I proceeded to the great Drift of Snow, that lay right across the Canal, at Ardclough hill, and where great exertion had been made on Tuesday, by which one of the Fly Boats were literally dragged over, and through the snow, for several perches—it is scarcely credible, but nevertheless it is a positive fact, that the Drift filled in the entire bed of the Canal.

There was a steady increase in passengers after 1834, but it is interesting that this increase was largely accounted for by the night boats:

Year ending April	State cabin		Common cabin		
	day boat	night boat	day boat	night boat	Total
1833	6,200	5,396	21,652	21,566	54,814
1835	6,951	9,217	23,861	32,719	72,748
1837	9,614	17,311	26,624	47,146	100,695

Stokes submitted frequent reports complaining about the damage being inflicted to the banks by the team of galloping horses and the surge of the fly boats, whose wash swept right over the banks in places. He estimated that the damage and loss of water far outweighed the small increase in revenue. The company also incurred the expenditure of providing increased stable accommodation.

It will be recalled that Messrs Hartley & Desmond had damaged the company's passage boat business by starting a coach service from Dublin to Athlone. They soon extended this coach to Ballinasloe and Galway and in 1830 Daniel Desmond offered to rent the whole passage boat establishment from the company, but his offer was rejected. In 1835, however, the company was forced to come to terms with him and an agreement was worked out whereby Desmond promised to run a coach between Ballinasloe and Galway to connect with the passage boats.

The introduction of the fast boat services encouraged other coach operators to establish services in conjunction with them. The company subsidised coaches from Carlow to Athy, Mountmellick to Mountrath and Mountmellick to Abbeyleix via Maryborough (Portlaoise), free transport being provided between the Blundell aqueduct and Edenderry and between Stradbally and Vicarstown.

In 1836 Charles Bianconi approached the company with a view to arranging services to meet the boats. By this time he had extended his services north and west from Clonmel and had cars operating from Roscrea to Ballinasloe.[2] In characteristic fashion, he immediately set about establishing a personal relationship with the directors and waited upon the board whenever he wished to discuss matters of importance. He agreed to commence a service between Ballinasloe and Galway with the possibility of opening up a service to Tuam in the future. He was to receive a fixed bounty of £250 per annum with an increase of £200 when the Tuam car commenced. Shortly after this meeting he wrote to the board from Clonmel in connection with the insertion of a three-year clause in his contract. He referred to his rivals Hartley & Desmond, whom the canal company had now forsaken for him:

> Not acquainted with the Constitution of your Board, and least the threats of the great Coach monopoly at present existing, should gain the preponderance in your Board hereafter, as to sacrifice me to their rapacity, and if anything were wanted in addition to their opposition to your former contractor I would refer you to the extraordinary correspondence with myself and in fair competition, I would compare their best efforts against us, as one biting a sharp file.

Within a year Bianconi had extended his Tuam car to Castlebar and had agreed to run a car from Roscrea to Shannon Harbour. All these routes he operated with his well-known open cars at a standard rate of 1½d per mile. Shortly after this he transferred his Birr car to meet the canal at Gallen, putting another coach operator on this route out of business. William Jessop junior had been operating a coach from Gallen to Birr since 1833, subsidised by the canal company, but Bianconi remarked that it was 'badly appointed'. After a few years he found that this route was not a success and he transferred the cars to the Kilbeggan–Athlone run. The company agreed to pay him a bounty of £100 per year for this route with an additional £40 for turnpike tolls. At the same time the board asked him to stop running his cars from Athlone to the Royal Canal, but there is no record whether he complied with this request.

When the serious breaches occurred on the Ballinasloe

Canal, he immediately stepped in to offer the company the use of some of his 'long cars' to convey the passengers by road to and from Shannon Harbour, 'which the horses now drawing the boats can conveniently work—these Cars take from sixteen to twenty Passengers each and four horses can draw them. If I can be in this or any other way serviceable to your Board, I request they may freely command me.' He was able to perform another service which must have appealed to his keen business sense. He agreed with Bagot that he would take over the horse contracts on the canal at a lower figure, thereby forcing the horse contractors, who had been refusing to accept a reduction in their rates, to comply with the company's proposals.

In 1840 it was reported that he was carrying over 10,000 passengers a year on his three principal routes connected with the canal, from Athlone, Galway and Castlebar. By 1844 he had extended his cars to Ennis and Westport and was receiving over £900 per year in bounties from the canal company, which was paying another £700 per year in bounties to other coach operators. In that year, 1844, a rival company commenced to operate coaches from Dublin to Roscrea and Carlow and the canal company had to increase its bounties and reduce fares to meet this opposition. It was reported of the Carlow coach that they were prepared to accept very low fares 'rarely refusing what a passenger will offer'. By this time the fare to Shannon Harbour from Dublin had been reduced to 11s (55p) state or 7s 6d (37½p) common cabin by the day boat and 10s (50p) or 6s 8d (33½p) by the slower night boat. The number of passengers rose steadily, reaching a peak of 120,615 in 1846; the revenue from the passage boats, however, did not reflect this increase because of the reductions in fares, rising from £23,634 in 1840 to £25,654 in 1845.

In addition to the opposition from the coach operators, the railways were about to present a new threat and to force the canal company to make further reductions in fares. It soon became obvious that water transport was going to find it very difficult to compete with the railways for passenger traffic. In

1847, as part of an agreement with the GS & WR, whose line to the south followed the Grand Canal closely from Dublin to Sallins, it was arranged that all boats (except the night boats) from Dublin to Sallins would cease to operate and the passengers would travel by rail to Sallins and there transfer to the boats. The railway company, aware of its strength, was very uncooperative about the timetable and annoyed the canal company by substituting uncovered waggons for the canal passengers, 'thereby exposing the Passengers to all the inclemency of the weather'. As this occurred in the month of January, the canal company protested in strong terms and covered carriages were restored after two weeks.

The end was in sight. In 1848 the canal company warned Bianconi that his bounties would have to be reduced and shortly after this they were withdrawn. Bianconi, typically, did not fight the railways, 'I see that the railways must be made; and I do not oppose them but I have taken shares in the undertaking'.[3] He bought up some of the coaching establishments like Hartley & Desmond, who were afraid to face the future, and set about reorganising his business in co-operation with his new competitor.

The passage boat establishment was gradually reduced. The swift boats to Athy and Mountmellick ceased on 31 March 1847 and the night boat on 3 June. The intermediate boat from Ballycommon to Ballinasloe was withdrawn on 5 December and on 1 January 1848 the service to Kilbeggan was terminated. The company had to compensate the horse contractors for the early termination of their contracts. In that year nine swift boats and two heavy boats were sold, some of them fetching as little as £12.

The remaining services, the day boat from Sallins to Ballinasloe and the night boat from Dublin to Ballinasloe, still managed to show a profit and in a last despairing effort the directors decided to build two twin screw passage boats which would accommodate 100 passengers each. The hulls were built by Barrington of Ringsend for £230 each and the engines, with oscillating cylinders, were supplied by Inshaw of Birmingham for £475 each. By the time these boats were ready the company had carried out some experiments with screw steamers which will be described in Chapter 8, and found that they were not very satisfactory in the narrow confines of the canal. Fares had by this time been reduced several times to compete with railway opposition. The journey from Dublin to Ballinasloe, which was now competing with the new railway to Galway, could be made for 5s (25p) state or 3s 6d (17½p) common cabin. The board decided to give up the unequal struggle and on 5 October 1852 the service from Shannon Harbour to Ballinasloe was terminated and all boats ceased to operate on 31 December. The new passage boats never carried passengers; they were used as towing steamers for a short time; then the engines were sold and the hulls converted into trade boats.

In order to follow the passage boats to their conclusion it has been necessary to move ahead in time, but, when the overall effect of the railways is considered in Chapter 8, it will be seen that the decision to terminate the passage boats was influenced by the negotiations which were in progress at this time with the railway companies.

It now remains to consider the company's five hotels at Sallins, Robertstown, Tullamore, Portobello and Shannon Harbour. They were not a financial success; they cost the company nearly £30,000 to build, furnish and maintain up to 1812 and they produced very little return for this outlay.[4] Improved coaching connections and the increasing demand by travellers to reach their destinations as quickly as possible, made these large hotels unnecessary.

John Byron was the first tenant of the hotel at Sallins which was completed in 1784, but he did not lease it for very long, because in 1792 it was reported that the hotel 'lately occupied by Smyth' was now vacant. The board advertised it pointing out that the passage boats stopped there and 'being in the neighbourhood of Mr Ponsonby's foxhounds render it peculiarly eligible for any person wishing to engage in the tavern business'. Mrs Waterson took it over but by 1802 it was again vacant. It was obvious that it was too close to Dublin to be of any significant advantage to the passage boats, and three years later it was still vacant 'with a quantity of fowl feeding in the best parlours'. In 1806 David Courtney, a Dublin flour miller, leased it for 999 years with a clause which bound him to put it into repair with a minimum outlay of £500 within one year. It is not clear whether he operated it as a hotel but, when he died in 1812, a lengthy legal argument started with his representatives who tried to surrender the lease. By this time the building was in very bad repair and the company disputed whether the repair clause had been fulfilled.

For some years there was no official tenant although it was occupied occasionally by squatters; one group was ejected in 1832. Then from 1844 until 1847 the GS & WR leased it while the railway was being constructed. The Daly family were the next tenants. They looked after the maintenance of sections of the banks and trackways for the company under contract and later became the horse contractors for the company's trade boats. In 1893 the company took possession of the building for non-payment of rent and four years later it was leased to Mr Hanlon at £30 per annum on a long lease. It is used today as a factory by Premier Meat Packers (Ireland) Ltd.

In the 1790s there was a hotel at Athy and Mr Molyneaux opened one at Monasterevan in 1796 which catered for canal passengers but there is no evidence that these were company hotels, although the house at Monasterevan was later occupied by the company's agent. There is a local tradition that the ruined house at Stacumney was once a hotel but this is probably because rooms were rented in it in the 1780s during the season for drinking the waters at the nearby Lucan spa. One of the company's buildings at Philipstown (Daingean) was also used as a hotel for a short period in the 1790s.

In 1796 James Oates submitted plans for a hotel at Lowtown but the scheme was not finally approved until 1799, and the site ultimately chosen was in the nearby village of Robertstown. William Semple won the contract and commenced work that year. Before long it was reported to the board that he was using bad materials for the masonry work and 'the walls are erecting in a slovenly, imperfect and unsafe manner'. Two years later the hotel was still unfinished and Semple was warned that he had exceeded the time specified in his contract. He blamed the company's choice of site which had provided a very poor foundation, so that he had been forced to remove an 18in crust and use planks to form a solid base at the west end. Shortly after this he was declared a bankrupt but John Semple agreed to complete the work. In August 1801 he reported that the building was ready and the board ordered it to be furnished 'in a neat, plain and substantial manner'. The company decided to run this hotel itself and Allen McMillan, a former passage boat captain, was appointed hotelkeeper. His wages were £1 2s 9d (Ir) per week but he was to receive a bonus of 26 guineas (Ir) every six months following an inspection of the house and furniture.

It was not long before the complaints started. McMillan was ill for some time and 'great irregularities' were reported. Mr Grace of Chancery Lane complained that his maidservant had been put into the same room as himself and his wife and 'without sheets', and that, when he had refused to pay the full account, his luggage was seized. Business must have been good in these early days because the attic, in which the great clock stood, was converted into a bedroom for the maids and an extension wing was approved. Michael Morrin was the contractor; he was also criticised for using bad materials although he said he was using stone from Gollierstown, lime from Ballyteague and sand from Sallins. The extension took two years to complete and was opened in July 1804.

The complaints continued but McMillan remained in charge until his death in 1808 when he was succeeded by John Farrell. Business must have been declining because, when the board heard in 1811 that the military authorities were contemplating the establishment of a barracks at the Curragh, it was suggested that the hotel might be suitable, but the offer was declined.

The new board, elected in 1810, had carried out retrenchments in every department and Robertstown did not escape. The expenditure account was cut from £453 (Ir) to £203 (Ir) by reducing Farrell's wages to £1 10s (Ir) per week, cutting the turf and candles allowance and blocking up 27 windows and hearths to avoid tax. Further efforts were made to persuade the government to acquire the hotel but the military authorities said that they did not like 'the damp and aguish nature of the neighbouring country'. The company replied 'on the contrary that from the circumstances of the hotel being erected on the Summit Level of the Grand Canal, it is distinguished for its Salubrity, and on this subject the Directors beg leave to express their wish for a reference to some medical person or persons to report thereon'. In 1813 the expenditure account was reduced further and only 31 windows and 19 hearths were retained, reducing the number of sleeping apartments to 11.

Nicholas Whyte leased the hotel in 1815 for £26 (Ir) per annum in addition to all taxes and licences. Farrell was told he must leave and Whyte took over the company's furniture at a valuation of £406 (Ir). Nicholas Whyte died in 1827 and, as already mentioned, his brother, Robert, took over his lease of the hotel. Robert's account books provide a very good picture of life in the hotel, the servants employed with their wages and duties, the expenses involved in clothing and educating his family and other interesting details including a 'Receipt for making Barm' given to Mrs Whyte by a Miss Kent.[5] There do not appear to have been many guests, although the hotel was used by the company's officers and by the directors on their annual inspection; sometimes people engaged a suite of rooms for quite long periods. A number of diocesan conferences were held there in the 1820s; on one such occasion dinner for 21 people cost £2 12s 6d (£2.62½) with an additional 19s 6d (97½p) for punch and 2s 4d (11½p) for porter for the drivers. Robert died in 1844 and his widow was left with four young children. She remained in the hotel and continued to fulfil her husband's horse contract until it expired in 1846. In December of the following year Mrs Whyte was given notice to quit despite the fact that she had paid her rent regularly. The board later relented but she must have been uncertain of her tenure because she surrendered the hotel in 1849.

The company soon found a new tenant. Jasper Rogers and his two sisters took over the building in 1850 and thereafter it ceased to be a hotel. Rogers was in charge of the Irish Amelioration Society's work on the nearby bog at Derrymullen and he wanted a residence and offices. A section of bog had been leased in 1848 and it was intended to set up a manufactory of peat charcoal. It is worth noting that C. W. Williams had developed this idea some years earlier. He had tried to obtain premises from the canal company at Shannon Harbour in 1838 but finally he set up his works on the Royal Canal at Cappoge where he produced a form of compressed peat and also experimented with peat charcoal, neither of which were a financial success.[6]

The Amelioration Society held a 'grand official opening' in September 1850 which is described in detail in the *Illustrated London News*:

> Shortly after six o'clock, such of the company as had to return to Dublin betook themselves again to the canal boats. . . . In the evening, Mr J. W. Rogers, whose residence, Peat House, Robertstown, was brilliantly illuminated, gave a ball and party to such of the directors and managers as remained in town.

The society ceased production after a few years and Rogers went to England, but his sisters stayed on for a time and the hotel was not surrendered until 1867.

Two years later, 'after considerable negotiation' the Royal Irish Constabulary agreed to lease the building as a barracks at an annual rent of £42. Part of the house was converted into a residence for the district inspector and the RIC continued to use the premises for many years, finally surrendering it in 1905. Mrs Hughes then took a lease of the DI's residence but, apart from occasional tenants who rented rooms, the rest of the building was not used again until the government took it over from 1942–8 to house men engaged in a turf cutting scheme. It was used as a youth hostel from 1951–4 and in recent years it has become a centre for the local branch of Muintir na Tire (a community organisation) and their efforts, inspired by Father P. J. Murphy, in preserving the hotel as a canal museum and in organising period banquets and an annual canal 'Festa' are well known.

The directors decided to build a hotel in Tullamore in 1800 because there was no accommodation available in the town. Michael Hayes, one of the canal contractors, built it within a year and it was opened to the public by the end of 1801. George Forrest leased it for six years but then surrendered it because he said that the alteration in the passage boat time-table had deprived him of all his business. Hotelkeepers ran the hotel for the company for the next few years until Andrew Morgan, who was acting as hotelkeeper at the time, leased it in 1815 for £52 per year. He advertised it in glowing terms:

> To such as take the Boat his House claims a decided preference; as it precludes every disappointment; the Apartments are fitted up with neatness and elegance; Beds constantly aired; Good Dinners and excellent wines, Carriages and Jaunting Cars, and Careful Drivers at reduced prices.

Business steadily declined in the 1820s and by 1834 Morgan reported that he had no customers 'apart from a few breakfasts'. He surrendered his lease and Miss Purcell took it over; but by 1838 it was in bad repair and generally empty. She was persuaded to surrender and there followed a series of short tenancies including the MGWR. Finally in 1859 the Rev McAlroy, the local parish priest, leased the hotel from the company and it is still used as the presbytery today.

In 1805 the board decided to build a hotel at Portobello on the Circular Line and to make this the terminus of the passage boats instead of James's Street Harbour. Thomas Colbourne, one of the company's engineers, drew up the plans and

Alexander Wilson won the contract with his quotation of £5,049 (Ir). Cut stone was brought from Tullamore, slates from Killaloe and marble from Clononey for the mantelpieces which cost £5 2s 3d (Ir) each to make. It was furnished and ready to receive guests by 13 July 1807; the furnishings had cost £841 (Ir).

As already mentioned Philip Weekes died before he could take up his appointment but his widow and son became the hotelkeepers. They were not very efficient and soon owed the company a great deal of money. In 1810 the board decided to lease the hotel to George Whitley for £520 (Ir) per annum and Mrs Weekes and her son were given notice. Whitley was constantly in financial difficulties and even though the board reduced his rent his goods were seized and auctioned to pay his debts and he had to surrender his lease in 1817.

In 1818 James Heron, a retired passage-boat captain, rented the hotel for £6 (Ir) per week and he appears to have run a well-

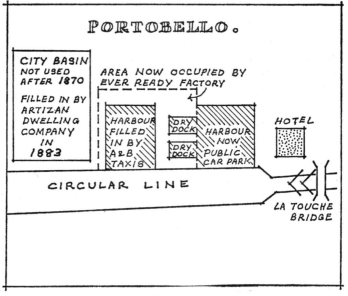

FIGURE 18

conducted establishment. A Dublin guide book in 1821 des-
cribes it as 'fitted up with elegance for the accommodation of
families and single gentlemen. The beauty and salubrity of the
situation enlivened by the daily arrival and departure of the
canal boats, render it a truly delightful residence'.[7] When he
died in 1831, his son George took over but decided to surrender
his lease in 1835. He asked that the interest on his father's bond
should be waived, pointing out all the improvements that had
been carried out and adding that it was still 'one of the best
conducted and quietest hotels in Dublin for a family one'.

George Heron must have realised that business was declining
because Thomas Wilkinson, the next tenant, complained after
one year that he frequently had an empty house. The board
refused to reduce his rent, which was only £4 per week, but
he was allowed a rebate to carry out essential repairs. He died
in 1843 and his widow continued to manage the hotel, but
after 1846 the railways began to reduce the numbers of passengers travelling by water and she was allowed several rent
reductions, until by 1848 she was paying £100 per year. She
surrendered her lease in 1855 and emigrated with her family.

Peter Ryan, the next tenant, took a 99-year lease and sublet
the premises as a blind asylum, which it remained until 1868
when the lease was surrendered. For the next twenty years the
company had a series of unsatisfactory tenants. By this time
the building was in very bad repair, the roof was neglected
and the windows had been broken by boys. Finally, in 1896
Miss Hampson took over the premises at a rent of £110 per
annum for 'use as a Private Hospital'. She undertook to spend
£500 in repairs and in the years that followed it continued to
be used as a private nursing home. New leases were negotiated
and further improvements carried out. In 1971 the nursing
home closed down and the new owners intend to convert the
building into offices.

Before leaving the subject of Portobello it is worth noting a
few details about the area beside the hotel. It was a place of
great activity in the days of the passage boats with two har-

bours and two dry-docks. It is amusing to record that in 1819 a fine of £1 (Ir) was levied on any captain who was found dumping rubbish in the harbours because it was alleged that rubbish and bottles rose to a height of 4ft from the bottom. A city basin had been constructed here in 1806 to supplement the water supply, but it ceased to be used in 1870 and in 1883 the Artizan Dwelling Company built on this area. They tried to lease some of the adjoining ground from the Grand Canal Company 'used as it now is for filthy and immoral purposes' but the request was turned down. In 1912 some of the wharves and the disused harbour area were leased to the Waytes who established the firm A & B Taxis, Dublin's first taxi service. In 1930 Armstrong Siddeley took over their premises and they were allowed to sell their lease to Ever-Ready in 1935, when the board was assured that the manufacture of batteries would not be 'noisy or offensive'. They extended their lease to occupy the remaining area, except the second harbour which was filled in by Dublin Corporation a few years ago to make a public car park.

Portobello lock has claimed more victims then any other Grand Canal lock. A soldier was drowned in it in 1824 because the lock-keeper refused to lend his drag to rescue him; he told them 'they might go to hell for a drag, that if his was at home, he would not lend it to save any soldier'. The lock claimed six more lives on the night of 6 April 1861, when a horse-drawn bus, bound for the city from Rathmines, mounted the bridge and rolled backwards into the lock.[8] Four more people were drowned in 1940 when a car was accidentally driven into it.

Shannon Harbour Hotel, built by the canal contractor David Henry, was completed in 1806. Although the other hotels were doing well at this time, this hotel was not a success. Luke Harton, the first tenant, surrendered before his three-year lease expired because 'he thinks it hard that He should pay the rent and keep servants in it and nothing doing'. The company appointed a hotelkeeper, John Clooney, who was instructed to operate it as a limited establishment with six bedrooms and two

Page 139 The horse ferry at Shannon Harbour in 1894. It replaced a wooden bridge in 1849; (*below*) Clonbrock Farm, Doonane, 1971; the gateposts are made from the shaft of one of the colliery pumps

Page 140 The canal in 1894; (above) a Priestman grab dredger working at Ticknevin; (below) Shannon Harbour

reception rooms. Windows and hearths were closed up until by 1814 there were only twenty-four windows and fifteen hearths left open. In 1825 James Egan leased it for £25 (Ir) per year and the directors visiting it on their annual inspection 'approved highly of the manner in which Mr Egan is fulfilling his engagements respecting it'. By 1829, however, he was forced to give it up because he owed a year's rent and 'he and his family are very much distressed'.

By 1833 the hotel was reported to be in 'a shameful state of decay' but new tenants were found in the following year, Mr and Mrs Moore, who stayed for two years. There is an interesting reference to the hotel in an unpublished account of a journey down the canal in 1836 written by F. S. Bourke: 'There is a very spacious hotel at Shannon Harbour, which is said to afford excellent accommodation.' He went on, however, to say that he spent the night with friends in Banagher, 'and I would strongly advise all persons, gentle and simple, who travel that way, to do the same if they can'.[9]

John Falkner, the next tenant, was soon doing a good business with the growing tide of emigration and the introduction of the fast day boats. James Larkin, one of the company's agents in the 1920s, wrote a description of the harbour in these busy days as recounted to him by some of the old people of the area.[10] He said that every house in the village had to take in lodgers because the hotel was not large enough to accommodate all the travellers. The place was full of excitement with singing and dancing to the music of the bagpipes and flute provided by travelling musicians.

By 1843 the hotel business was declining, so Falkner sold his furniture and closed the hotel. Joshua Gill tried to continue it as a hotel but abandoned it after three years and the next tenant, Pat Rorke, reported in 1847 that business had gradually diminished. The board allowed him to continue to occupy the hotel as caretaker, some of the rooms being rented to canal employees and traders. The company had a fitting shop in the store beside the dry docks but this was closed down in 1925

I

and the plant and machinery moved to Dublin. The hotel building was allowed to deteriorate and finally the remaining tenants were found alternative accommodation in the old police barracks and the hotel was rendered uninhabitable to avoid the payment of further rates.

CHAPTER 7

The Collieries and the
Middle Shannon

In the early 1800s the company undertook two ventures which
were to prove very costly in terms of both money and time.
These were the leasing of some collieries near Castlecomer, on
the borders of Queen's County (Leix) and County Kilkenny,
and the acquisition of the control and maintenance of the
middle Shannon.

In 1803 John Macartney and Richard Griffith decided that
the best method of building up a trade in coal on the canal was
for the company to acquire a colliery. Israel Rhodes, an
'eminent engineer' from England, who had come to Ireland
in 1802 to carry out some surveys for the company, was asked
to investigate the position. He wrote an enthusiastic report
suggesting the leasing of the Doonane collieries and the construction of a branch canal from Athy into the heart of the
mines, which would not only act as drainage but would bring
transport to the coalface. He produced lengthy statistics on the
amount of coal available, the tolls that would be charged and
the profits that would accrue to the company.

Macartney and Griffith then revealed that they had taken a
lease of the area for 41 years at an annual rent of £1,000
which they offered to assign to the company. It was subsequently alleged in 1810 that they had leased the collieries and
then, realising that they were not going to prove a successful
venture, had persuaded the board to take them over.[1] Griffith

said that this was 'a very scandalous and, as you well know, a perfectly unfounded story' and he explained that they had taken the lease in their names in the first instance because they feared that the proprietors would have increased the rent if they knew that the canal company was involved. Certainly in the light of Rhodes's report the board's decision to accept the offer of the lease seemed a sensible one at the time.

The collieries in the vicinity of Castlecomer had been worked for about a century before this but the profits had been small.[2] One colliery, inherited by Lady Ormonde from her father, Lord Wandesforde, had made an annual profit of up to £7,000 at times, though it had been less successful in the early 1800s. The colliery acquired by the canal company did not have a very good record.[3] In the early 1700s it had been leased for £600 per annum, but 'a Judicious Collier' estimated that every acre was worth a clear profit of £1,000. In 1794 young Robert Hartpole, the owner of the colliery who had recently married and was in financial difficulties, was advised that the collieries could be made to produce a profit of £6,000 per annum if properly managed. He decided, however, in November of that year, to lease them to James Dillon and William Billing of Dublin for £1,000 per year.

Rhodes, who does not seem to have had any mining experience, was placed in charge of the new venture and continued to write enthusiastic reports. He said that the determination of how best to work the collieries on an extensive scale was the most important subject that had ever claimed the attention of the board. He suggested the construction of a small drainage tunnel in the first instance which could later be enlarged to take boats. His estimated cost of obtaining a new steam engine and sinking and preparing ten pits would be about £20,000 (Ir) but, as each of these pits would then produce up to 7,000 tons of coal per year, the return would be considerable; he said there would be a clear profit of 12s (Ir) per ton on the coal, transported and sold in Dublin, with an even greater margin of profit when the branch canal was completed.

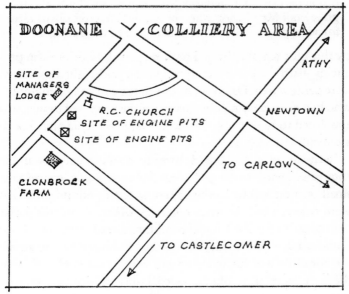

FIGURE 19

In addition to leasing the collieries, the company had taken over the 500-acre Clonbrock farm which was included in the area, the rent being £500 (Ir) pa. Over £2,000 was spent improving it with the intention of letting it but, when it did not prove a financial burden, the company continued to run it and the house was subsequently used by the colliery manager instead of the 'Lodge'.

One of the men employed by Rhodes, James Ryan, invented a new apparatus for boring and the company lent him £120 to enable him to take out a patent.[4] Ryan was apparently a man of difficult temperament and Rhodes referred to his 'wildness and total want of experience'. When Rhodes decided to return to England in November 1804, Ryan was outspoken about it to the board:

> I fear from the expence attending the speculative trials, and no profit arising to cover them, the concern will accumulate a debt

that in the end will ruin the undertaking; who will have the disgrace? not Mr Rhodes, who got off, but the professional men found in your service at the winding up of the business.

By this time ten old pits had been reopened, some of them producing hard coal, the others soft coal, and eight new shafts were being bored. David Aher, one of the company's engineers, who had been carrying out surveys of the proposed tunnel, was appointed to replace Rhodes, which angered Ryan and created a difficult atmosphere.

Early in 1805 the board, already disillusioned about the enterprise, tried to let the collieries as a going concern. A small portion was let to the adjoining tenant but no proposals were received for the main collieries which would reimburse the company for the large expenditure already incurred. Lord Dundonald, a mining expert, was asked to come over to advise the company and his reports were very gloomy. He said that the best method of obtaining coal was by sinking pits and using a steam engine to unwater them; he could find no purpose in constructing a tunnel, 'the very reverse was the case—such a tunnel could not be completed during the term of the company's lease of the Collieries, and at an expence, double that stated in his [Rhodes's] estimate'. The company, he added, had been misled by Rhodes's 'hastily adopted ideas of a tunnel, based on the supposition that there was coal to be found everywhere on the Royalties'. He estimated that the maximum amount of coal available was 2,400,000 tons and a great number of the trial pits could be abandoned. He dismissed Ryan's invention which, he said, had been practised in Scotland twenty-five years ago and was not considered as successful as the old method. He concluded by suggesting that 'a practical collier' should be appointed to manage the concern.

Ryan was dismissed and the board decided to seek a second opinion, hoping that Lord Dundonald's conclusions might prove inaccurate. W. B. Davies of Neston, Cheshire, agreed to come over; his report repeated most of the same recommendations. In June 1805 the board was forced to call a special general meeting about the collieries in response to a requisition from some of the proprietors. The directors had to admit that £80,340 (Ir) had been spent on developing the collieries and £5,591 (Ir) on the farm with very little return, but they stressed 'the novel and arduous nature of the business'. A third opinion was sought and William Dixon, of Govan colliery near Glasgow, was paid £150 and his expenses to prepare a report. He repeated much of what had been said in the other reports and stressed the importance of a 'skilful manager'. 'With respect to the plans of tunnels and drifts', he added, 'they appear to me the most extravagant that I ever before have heard of.' Neither the drift not the tunnel were attempted, nor was the suggestion pursued that a railway to Athy might be constructed, but a small amount of money was spent instead on improving the road from Doonane to Athy, and the coal continued to be brought to the canal by carriers.

David Aher resigned in 1805 to become manager of Lady Ormonde's colliery and in December Andrew Faulds, a mining engineer from Scotland, agreed to become manager at a salary of 300 guineas (Ir) per year with a free house for himself and his family. His first recommendation was that work should be continued on three pits where coal had been definitely established and that a steam engine should be purchased from Scotland immediately. He tried to show an interest in the welfare of his colliers but, ironically, he was the first manager to have trouble with the workers. This arose because he tried to introduce the Scottish system of working in the pits which involved paying the men by the ton instead of the Irish custom of paying a weekly wage. He reported a 'strong spirit of combination which it is absolutely necessary to supress' and by September 1806 he had a full-scale strike on his hands: 'the colliers has made a combination rather to starve than allow any new mode of working to be introduced.'

Faulds broke the strike after a few weeks and the men agreed to work by the ton but a dispute then arose as to how much per ton they should be paid. Faulds reported to the board that a large crowd assembled and tried to force terms on him but he refused to give in to this intimidation. The board supported his stand but the situation worsened and he described in vivid terms how he had to face a hostile and drunken crowd:

> There was not a moment's time to be lost for it was hard to say what the mob would have proceeded to next—I was unarmed but I told them I would instantly charge thro' them on my horse and beat out as many of their brains as I could if they did not immediately disperse, which had the desired effect.

The board asked the military authorities to send a detachment to Doonane and Faulds was given permission to bring over six young Scottish miners. With their help he managed to get one pit working and to train some young Irishmen so that gradually more pits were reopened. The old miners held out, although some of them returned to work when they were threatened with eviction from the houses which the company had built for them.

When some members of the board visited Doonane in 1807 in the course of their annual inspection, they found that Faulds was paying only half the wages of the neighbouring colliery and the margin of profit per ton was quite high, approximately £1 per ton transported and sold in Athy. The board decided that it would be an advantage to have a coal yard at Lowtown and this was put in hand and completed by 1808. In May of that year Faulds reported that the new engine pit had been completed to the coal level, but in the next report he said that he was having difficulty with the leather drive of the steam engine, which was not yet working. He added that his relations with the people were improving; their distress had been so great he had purchased potatoes for them 'and according as I got their wants supplied, the people are turning out to their Work with seeming Gratitude'. The board, ignoring this part of his report, replied that it had received the news about the engine 'with much regret and Disappointment'. Faulds was justifiably angry and said that had he known of the difficulties of the undertaking, no sum would have tempted him to accept the position. There followed an exchange of letters and, in June 1808, the directors, their patience exhausted, accepted his resignation.

Renewed efforts were made to let the concern and John Killaly was asked to go to Doonane to report on the situation. His report suggested that the board had been hasty in accepting the resignation of Faulds who, he considered, displayed 'a strong understanding and a minute knowledge of Colliery affairs'. Killaly threatened to resign if he was asked to take over the position of manager, but during his short stay he sent in some detailed reports which show the position at the collieries at that time. Five pits were being worked, two more were being excavated and over 100 men were being employed, but he said it was difficult to obtain the maximum effort from these men who appeared to be naturally idle. In the years 1806–8 the total revenue had amounted to £15,242 but the expenses for the same period were £23,208.

Killaly was relieved by Thomas Colbourne, another of the company's engineers; there is no evidence that he had any mining experience. He reported a growing discontent among the workers who were living in very bad conditions and were dissatisfied with their earnings. He experienced a great deal of trouble but he did manage to keep some of the pits working. By this time one board meeting each week was set aside to be devoted to the problems of the collieries, and efforts to dispose of the whole undertaking were continued. Finally, in 1810 Colbourne sent in his resignation and the board considered suspending all work. It was suggested to Colbourne that he should let it be known that work would be discontinued if full working was not resumed and, in the face of this threat, the colliers, who had been holding out for higher wages, returned to work.

Nicholas Ross, the company's storekeeper at James's Street, agreed to take over from Colbourne in October 1810. By this time, despite the labour troubles, the enormous capital outlay was beginning to show results and a profit was being realised each year. In the course of the government inquiry into the company's affairs in 1812 it was revealed that the expenditure on the collieries had been £95,372 (Ir), and the total revenue had amounted to £39,498 (Ir) thus showing a deficit of £55,874 (Ir).[5] Ross had been compelled to increase wages but in the year ending October 1811 he reported a profit of £5,283 (Ir). The fact that the colliery was showing a profit was a considerable help to the company in the government inquiry but, as already mentioned, they had to accept that the colliery profits must be used to pay off the debt and could not provide funds for a dividend.

Coalyards were opened at Ringsend and James's Street to help to work off some of the coal on bank, which had amounted to 4,000 tons in 1811. In April 1814 there was a new strike for higher wages and a military detachment was sent to Doonane to help Ross control the situation. Despite the strike, profits continued to rise, reaching £9,771 (Ir) in 1816, but thereafter sales began to fall as the years of depression set in. Nearly 400 men were now employed and, when Ross was told that he would have to reduce the quantity of coal raised, he said that it would produce great hardship to lay off men in their present distressed condition with rising food prices.

In 1819 Richard Griffith junior, who was by this time an established mining engineer,[6] was asked to inspect the collieries and report on what further searches for coal he would recommend. His report was very gloomy; he said that all the best coal had been worked out and he would not advise the expenditure of any money in searches for new seams. In their half-yearly report to the company in October 1820 the directors said, 'the cheapness of Turf, the scarcity of money and the almost total cessation of manufacturing enterprise' had reduced the sales in coal. The Doonane district had its share of disturbance at this time, Ribbonmen were active and the military detachment was increased to fifty men.

In 1823 the company tried unsuccessfully to surrender the lease and in the following year Mr McLaren, a Scottish mining engineer, who was visiting Ireland at the request of the Mining Company of Ireland, was asked for his advice. He criticised the methods used in working and unwatering the pits. He offered to arrange for a mining overseer from Scotland, Robert Nicholson, to come over to introduce reforms. Ross was not pleased about this and asked the board to return him to his position in Dublin, but Nicholson must have considered the problems too difficult because he returned to Scotland after a very short time.

The establishment was gradually reduced and by 1828 there was little hope of the revenue producing more than the rent and running costs. Ross repeatedly asked the directors to return him to Dublin, 'from a place where the better part of my life has been spent in their service, deprived of almost everything that could render it even tolerable'. There was little demand for coal or culm and the neighbourhood of Doonane was 'much disturbed'. Early in 1830 Ross reminded the board that it was now five years since he had first asked to be allowed to return to Dublin and twenty years since his arrival at the collieries, where he had 'spent his best days'. This time his request was granted; he returned to James's Street as collector and did not retire until 1847, when he was given an annuity of £120 but died a few weeks later.

John Edge, the cashier at the colliery, was appointed manager, but the board must have realised that the position was hopeless because it was decided to try once again to surrender the lease. On 1 May 1831 Maria Lecky and Martha Bowen, daughters of the late Robert Hartpole, accepted a surrender which included all the coal on bank, the engine and machinery, an assignment of all rents and a fine of £208. The costly and troublesome venture was at an end.

It is interesting that John Edge had arranged with the lessors to take over the collieries when the canal company surrendered.[7] His rent was reduced to £500 per year but with only a half share in the colliery profits. The lease was renewed in 1874 by Benjamin Booker Edge, presumably his son, who had been given the name of Benjamin Booker, pay clerk and land agent of the canal company for over forty years. Young Edge had to pay a rent of £250 per year with a royalty of 7d per ton on all coal sold, but he was not able to make a success of the concern and in 1883 he surrendered his lease of the colliery but retained his tenure of Clonbrock farm. It is doubtful if any further attempts were made to work the collieries and today there is scarcely any sign of all this former activity, although James Doyle, one of the old inhabitants, was able to recall stories of the days of Faulds, Ross and the Edges.

The company's other venture, the acquisition of the middle Shannon, was to prove equally difficult and non-productive. Some work, commencing in 1755, had been carried out to make the River Shannon navigable but, when William Chapman carried out a survey in 1791 at the request of the Limerick Navigation Company, he reported many deficiencies.[8] This report caused anxiety to the Grand Canal Company, which at that time was engaged in constructing the final stage of the canal to the Shannon. The board made a careful study of the report and approached the government with the suggestion that the company would be prepared to carry out improvements on the middle Shannon from Lough Derg to Lough Ree and maintain this section of the river if the necessary financial aid was authorised.[9] William Jessop carried out surveys of the whole river and produced estimates of the work which would be required and negotiations were commenced in 1800 with the Directors-General of Inland Navigation.

Discussions continued and in September 1801 the canal company's suggestion, that it should 'lay out a few hundred pounds on some of the locks', was approved by the directors-general. In November Jessop carried out another survey: this time he said that he was considering the work 'as a great National concern unfettered by local considerations or parsimonious frugality'. He recommended a navigation double the dimensions of the Grand Canal, envisaging the Shannon 'as the great Artery of Ireland, destined by future Ramifications to circulate its commerce and give animation to the Country'. His new estimates were nearly double his earlier ones, amounting to £119,454 for the Shannon north of Lough Ree and £55,821 for the middle Shannon. He stressed the importance of constructing trackways on the river as 'without them any other improvements of the Navigation would hardly be worth the cost of them'.

Israel Rhodes, who, as it has been seen, was shortly to encourage the company to embark on the colliery scheme, carried out a detailed survey of the river in 1802. He recommended the lowering of the cills of the locks at Athlone and Meelick and the construction of conventional locks at Shannonbridge and Banagher to replace the single sets of gates or rhymer locks there. He suggested that the river was so wide and devoid of shelter that it would never make a satisfactory navigation and the construction of a parallel canal would be more practical. Jessop said that he did not share these apprehensions, although it might be found easier to construct a parallel canal in some places.

It had now become a matter of some urgency; the Grand Canal was almost completed to Shannon Harbour and trade with Athlone and Limerick would be impossible with the river in its present condition. Unable to obtain a decision from the directors-general, the canal company went ahead with the reconstruction of the locks despite a warning that work on this large scale had never been sanctioned. Negotiations continued and, as has already been shown in Chapter 4, the company also suggested that it should carry out the necessary work to make the River Suck navigable to Ballinasloe. By this time the estimate for the work on the middle Shannon had risen to £112,000 (or £73,383 without trackways) because of rising costs and the 'unchecked spirit of combination among artificers and workmen of every denomination'. The canal company suggested that the directors-general should pay two-thirds of the cost and in return the toll on the completed navigation would be limited to 1d (Ir) per ton per mile.

The position remained unsatisfactory with no assurance of financial support forthcoming, but the company was now firmly embarked on the reconstruction work and reluctant to suspend operations. In September 1803 the board said that there would have to be a decision; Meelick lock had been virtually rebuilt and the work was proving very costly. At this point the directors-general tried to involve the question of tolls on the Grand Canal in the negotiations, but as already shown, the canal company insisted that this was a separate issue.[10] In October the board said that if it did not receive an assurance within one week that it would be reimbursed at least the £10,000 already expended, all work would be suspended and it would not spend 'another guinea in this work, but forthwith to remove all our Machinery and the Materials provided for the completion of it'. The directors-general agreed to negotiate a separate agreement about the tolls on the Grand Canal and work continued, but no solution was reached.

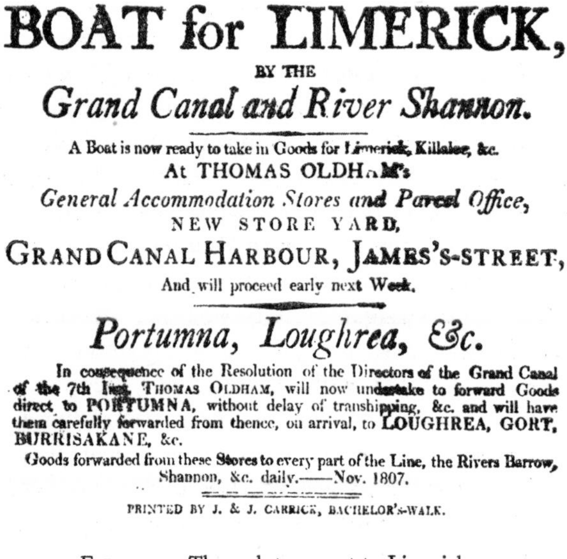

BOAT for LIMERICK,

BY THE
Grand Canal and River Shannon.

A Boat is now ready to take in Goods for Limerick, Killaloe, &c.
At THOMAS OLDHAM's
General Accommodation Stores and Parcel Office,
NEW STORE YARD,
GRAND CANAL HARBOUR, JAMES'S-STREET,
And will proceed early next Week.

Portumna, Loughrea, &c.

In consequence of the Resolution of the Directors of the Grand Canal of the 7th Inst. THOMAS OLDHAM, will now undertake to forward Goods direct to PORTUMNA, without delay of transhipping, &c. and will have them carefully forwarded from thence, on arrival, to LOUGHREA, GORT, BURRISAKANE, &c.

Goods forwarded from these Stores to every part of the Line, the Rivers Barrow, Shannon, &c. daily.——Nov. 1807.

PRINTED BY J. & J. CARRICK, BACHELOR'S-WALK.

FIGURE 20. Through transport to Limerick

Richard Griffith, the director who had supervised the completion of the Shannon Line, now transferred his attention to the work on the River Shannon. He reported that great difficulty was being experienced at Shannonbridge where, because of the close proximity of the short canal to the river, it was very difficult to keep out the water while the lock was being rebuilt. Work in sinking Athlone lock was slow and difficult and at Meelick, although the lock was finished, considerable slips in the banks were making the work of widening and deepening the canal much more difficult.

Negotiations with the directors-general were still making no progress and, in September 1804, the company threatened once again to suspend all work, pointing out that if the work was not completed before the winter set in, the navigation would remain closed until the following spring. The controversy dragged on, work ceased in December because of bad weather and in January 1805 the company wrote to the Lords of the Treasury informing them that no further work would be carried out and that the company was claiming compensation for all the money expended. In a letter to the directors-general the board said that it wished 'to put an end to this tedious and (to us) painful negotiation . . . the period for recommencing the work is at hand—on you alone depends whether the Navigation of the River Shannon shall be suffered to languish or be completed within the ensuing year, which great work we are capable of effecting if immediately favoured with a decisive answer'.

Finally, on 25 March 1806, an agreement was hammered out whereby the company was granted £54,634 for the reconstruction and maintenance of the middle Shannon. In August 1806 the Rt Hon Sackville Hamilton, chairman of the directors-general, visited the river and inspected the works from Portumna to Athlone. The company marked his visit by naming the rebuilt lock at Meelick, Hamilton lock. It is worth noting that all the locks rebuilt by the Grand Canal Company were subsequently abandoned when the major Shannon navigation works were carried out in the 1840s. At Athlone and Banagher the old canals and locks can still be traced; at Shannonbridge the small island and lock were removed but one side of the old lock forms the quay wall under the bridge, and at Hamilton lock some of Omer's original lock and the canal company's reconstruction work are clearly visible.

In July 1810 the company declared that the work had been completed and Killaly, accompanied by John Brownrigg for the directors-general, passed along the river in a boat drawing 5ft 9in. The Shannon was now navigable from Athlone to Killaloe but, because of a dispute between the Limerick Navigation Company and the directors-general, the canal from Killaloe to Limerick, damaged by floods in 1809, remained closed until 1814 despite the appeals of the Grand Canal Company and other interested parties.[11]

By 1817 it was reported that there were twenty-six trading boats operating on the river and through the canal to Dublin. Trading was very difficult on the river and very dependent on the weather. The canal company, uncertain about reimbursement, had abandoned the plan to construct towpaths and boats had to be sailed on the lakes and poled in the river, where the reed-covered banks made it impossible to haul them from the shore. As we have seen, the company showed a great interest in the development of steam boats and every encouragement was given to those who wanted to introduce steam navigation to the Shannon.

John Grantham, who had carried out a survey on flood control on the river with John Rennie in 1822, realised the potential of steam navigation. He bought a steamer in England and tried to set up a steam navigation company. He prepared a report for the Limerick Chamber of Commerce and approached the Grand Canal Company for a special reduction in tolls. Failing to gain government support, he offered to sell his steamer to the canal company but the directors replied that, although they were very interested in his venture, they did not wish to undertake the operation of the steamer because they

Page 157 Carrying: (*above*) clerical staff loading a boat at James's Street during the 1911 strike; (*below*) an M-boat approaching Healy or Bonynge Bridge near Robertstown, 1958

Page *158* Steam: (*above*) tug and train near Killina in 1894; (*below*) the *Bally-murtagh* Shannon steamer at Portumna about 1910

BALLYMURTAGH

GRAND CANAL.

Regular Parcel Boats to Athlone.

SAMUEL ROBINSON informs the ·Public that Goods sent to

THOMAS OLDHAM'S STORES,

Letter C.

NEW STORE YARD, GRAND CANAL HARBOUR,

JAMES's-STREET,

Will be regularly forwarded every Fortnight to *Samuel Robinson's* Stores in ATHLONE, by his Boats, which are provided with experienced, careful and respectable Captains; and the smallest damage immediately paid for, without litigation or unnecessary trouble.

S. ROBINSON will have the Goods carefully forwarded from ATHLONE, or stored there, (free of expense,) until sent for; any Goods sent to his Stores in ATHLONE for DUBLIN, will be forwarded in like manner.

NOV. 1807.

CARR... ... ...

FIGURE 21. Parcels to Athlone

understood that another company was building a steamer for the river. Grantham eventually decided to bring over his boat, the company agreeing to allow him to operate toll-free on the middle Shannon for the first year, with a bounty of 2s 6d (12½p) per passenger to or from Shannon Harbour. A memorial erected to Grantham in Killaloe cathedral states that he introduced steam navigation on the Shannon in 1825.[12] This, however, conflicts with the evidence in the records of the Grand Canal Company. Having reached agreement with the company, Grantham wrote to the board on 21 November 1826 to ask permission to put his steamer into the dry dock at Portobello, 'to take off some iron plates and clean her bottom from the effects of the salt water. That I wish to accomplish tomorrow that she may proceed to the Lake so as to arrive there before Sunday'. The reason for his haste was probably caused by the activities of the rival company, the Shannon Steam Navigation Company, who had approached the canal company for a pass for its steamboat, *Mountaineer*, on 24 October. There is no

K

evidence as to which of the boats actually reached the river first. The *Mountaineer* and Grantham's *Marquis Wellesley* are both mentioned once or twice more in the records of the canal company but little is known about the *Mountaineer*. An isolated rock in Lough Derg, called the 'Mountaineer rock', may explain her fate.

The canal company extended the remission of tolls to the other company, which soon built up its trade with stores at Portumna and Banagher. Grantham struggled on for a few years and then agreed to amalgamate with the larger concern. By 1832 he had broken off all connection with the steam company. In that year he entered into a contract with the canal company to plant willow and thorn trees on the exposed sections of the river, but he died in 1833 before he had completed his contract.

Charles Wye Williams, the principal director of the steam company, reached a new agreement with the canal company in 1829. Because he intended to enlarge his fleet, he was allowed to continue to operate toll-free on the river and at 1d per ton per mile on the canal for a further three years with a possible extension to seven years; the bounty on passengers was also continued. Two of his new steamers, the *Lady Clanricarde* and the *Dunally* arrived on the Shannon via the Grand Canal shortly after this and Williams also built up a fleet of horse-drawn trade boats on the canal which were towed by the steamers on the river. There is also a mention of his '*Wye* canal steamer' being delayed in the 33rd lock in April 1832, so it would appear that he used some steam power on the canal. He leased the redundant coal yard at Lowtown to provide stables and accommodation for his drivers.

Williams was anxious to see the Shannon Navigation improved and had published a pamphlet in 1831 suggesting that it would be a suitable scheme for the relief of the poor in the west of Ireland.[13] A commission was set up, which carried out a preliminary survey, and the government then decided to proceed with the scheme. In the course of these inquiries the

Grand Canal Company was accused of failing to observe the contract to maintain the middle Shannon and evidence was produced to show that the works had been allowed to fall into a bad state of repair.[14] Five Commissioners for the Improvement of the River Shannon were appointed in 1835 and set about their work without loss of time.

The canal company estimated that it should receive at least £50,000 compensation for the loss of the middle Shannon. It was pointed out to the commissioners that £30,273 had been spent over and above the original grant and, in addition, the company would now lose the revenue from tolls on the river, amounting to about £5,600 per year on about 20,000 tons carried on the middle Shannon. The commissioners awarded the company £5 and pointed out that they would be saved further expenditure in maintenance, while an increase in trade on the canal should follow the improvement of the Shannon.[15] The directors protested strongly and approached the Lords of the Treasury with the suggestion that the company would forgo the question of compensation if the Ballinasloe, Mountmellick and Kilbeggan canals were handed over.[16] As already shown, the government did eventually agree to hand over the branches in 1844, the outstanding loans being commuted to £10,000.[17]

In January 1840 the commissioners paid over the £5 and John Stokes, the company's engineer, was told to avoid 'any act which could on the one hand be construed or have the appearance of a voluntary surrender or abandonment of the company's rights in respect of the Navigation, or on the other of any opposition or interruption to the proceedings of the Commissioners'. Stokes carried out this difficult order admirably. A meeting took place between Major Jones, one of the commissioners, and Stokes at Athlone lock-house. They entered the house and Jones claimed it on behalf of the commissioners. 'I here remonstrated', Stokes reported to the board, 'that it could not be surrendered unless that kind of force were applied as to mark the proceedings against my consent, whereupon the Major applied his hand to the shoulder of the Lockkeeper his Wife and Child and also to your humble Servant and closed the Door upon us outside. He immediately readmitted the whole party and matters went on as before.' The same ceremony was repeated at the other lock-houses along the navigation and the official handing over 'under protest' was completed. Thus ended the company's years of control of the middle Shannon.

CHAPTER 8

The Famine and the Coming of the Railways

THE rapid increase in population in the early 1800s aggravated the problems of destitution among the poorer people and emigration became widespread. Numerous incidents were reported by passage-boat captains of trouble with the large crowds who assembled to speed the emigrants on their way. On one occasion, in April 1834, Richard Clooney described how his boat was boarded by an 'immense mob' at Shannon Harbour. He sent for military assistance and eventually proceeded to the double lock at Belmont:

> Notwithstanding that the Soldiers and Police had their Bayonets to the Common People they found their way thro' the lines formed and literally dashed their luggage down on the Boat when little better than half raised in the Lock and leaped on board in numbers after it, they then forced the boat out of the Lock.

The military were forced to 'read the Riot Act' and prepare to fire before the crowds accompanying the passengers were persuaded to disembark.

In 1839 the directors reported that a bad harvest had caused a decrease of over 6,000 tons in grain and flour carried by canal. Another bad harvest was reported in 1840 and the half-yearly report to the shareholders in April 1841 contains this interesting comment:

Another important fact connected with the subject arises out of the decided change which has taken place in the previous habits of a large portion of the People of this Country, which by enabling the Poor to become purchasers and consumers of Flour, Oatmeal etc to a much greater extent than formerly, has undoubtedly had the effect of decreasing the quantity of Corn bought up in distant Districts for the purpose of exportation and which was in many instances conveyed by Canal. We cannot doubt however that the general improvement of the Country consequent upon this important change, and the extension of both Trade and Agriculture growing out of it will speedily make good any deficiency arising from a cause otherwise so much to be rejoiced at.

In June 1840 the collector at Lowtown reported that he feared there would be a recurrence of attacks on trade boats, 'as the working classes throughout the district were in a state of great destitution owing to the want of employment and the high price of provisions'. Police patrols were set up and the trade boats were advised to spend the night where police protection was available. This effectively curbed the threatened trouble and in June 1842 similar action had to be taken. Bagot reported that flour had been pillaged from a boat at Ballyteague by a large mob: 'The state of the country and the wretched impoverished condition of the people justify the apprehension that such outrages will recur unless prompt and effective steps are taken.' He advised the reintroduction of the system of moving the boats in fleets with military protection. In a further report he said that subscriptions were being raised, 'the distress of the poor is so general and so urgent', and he asked for permission to give as much employment as possible in the poorer districts. The board agreed to this 'with due attention to economy and the interests of the Company'. A few months later he reported that he would be able to discontinue escorting the boats 'in consequence of the favourable expectations entertained of the state of the Harvest and the consequent peaceable disposition of the people of the Country'.

The impoverished state of the country each year in early

summer while awaiting the harvest, and the great distress which accompanied bad harvests, illustrates how very ill-equipped the country was to face the impending failure of the potato crop. Partial failures of this crop in 1817 and 1822 had caused widespread distress and another partial failure in 1845 caused Bagot to take steps once again to protect the trade boats:

> At the same time I am not disposed to fear that anything of the kind will soon occur, and probably it would be more prudent to write to the authorities simply drawing their attention to the subject, and the probability of disturbance should the prospect of scarcity become more evident and defined and requesting that they shall take such steps as they may deem requisite for ensuring the protection of the Trade.

By February 1846 the flood of emigrants was causing anxiety to the passage-boat captains. The board agreed to an application from the Commissary General, Sir R. J. Routh, to permit provisions to pass toll free 'to alleviate distress during the impending summer'.

In early summer 1846 it was reported that the 'pressure of want appears now to have subsided', and the secretary received a report that the local people of Edenderry 'by their promptitude, alacrity and good feeling' had averted serious damage from an accidental breach which occurred on the short branch canal to the town. The total failure of the potato crop in that year, however, soon plunged the country into renewed and even greater distress. The trade boats moved in convoys and the number of troops stationed along the canal was greatly increased. Starvation, disease and emigration decimated the population and, although the blight was not nearly so widespread in 1847, the crop was poor because so many of the seed potatoes had been eaten the year before.[1] In their half-yearly report to the company in 1847 the directors said that the normally large trade in corn into the city had been seriously affected and, although the trade out of the city had increased, it was 'clogged and encumbered with so many difficulties and embarrassments that it has been found impossible to carry it out to the extent which the wants of the country require'.

Tonnage figures for the years 1842–52 indicate the effect of the famine years on the company's trade (see Appendix 4).[2] In 1847 50,000 tons less than the previous year entered the city but an additional 20,000 tons left Dublin; the tonnage of grain increased from 438 tons in 1845 to 40,043 tons in 1847. The annual tonnage increased to over 280,000 tons in 1845–6 but it had fallen back to an average of about 230,000 tons by the 1850s.

The state of the country was not the only source of trouble for the directors; the increase in railway activity posed a far more serious threat to the prosperity of the company. In 1833 there had been some negotiations with the Dublin & Kingstown Railway Company regarding compensation for a railway embankment which would cross the canal basin at Ringsend; the railway agreed to pay £2,500 in addition to £348 compensation for permission to have a fixed arch instead of an opening span. The railway embankment virtually cut off the inner section of the basin to all except canal boat traffic, after which it was used to lay up old boats until, in the 1950s, it was eventually filled in.

This railway did not affect the company's traffic, but another, the Leinster & Munster, was planned on a directly competitive route; it was to run almost parallel with the canal to Sallins and turn southward to Kilkenny, thus serving the districts of the Barrow Line and the Barrow Navigation. The railway would have to cross the canal twice, near Sallins and on the Naas Line, and the canal company decided to object to these crossings in a petition to Parliament:

> Your Petitioners therefore humbly pray that no Legislative Sanction may be afforded to said project which although it will probably prove ultimately unsuccessful, threatens ruin in the meantime to a multitude of widows, orphans and fair creditors whose money has been advanced on the faith of Acts of Parliament promising to protect them against injurious competition.

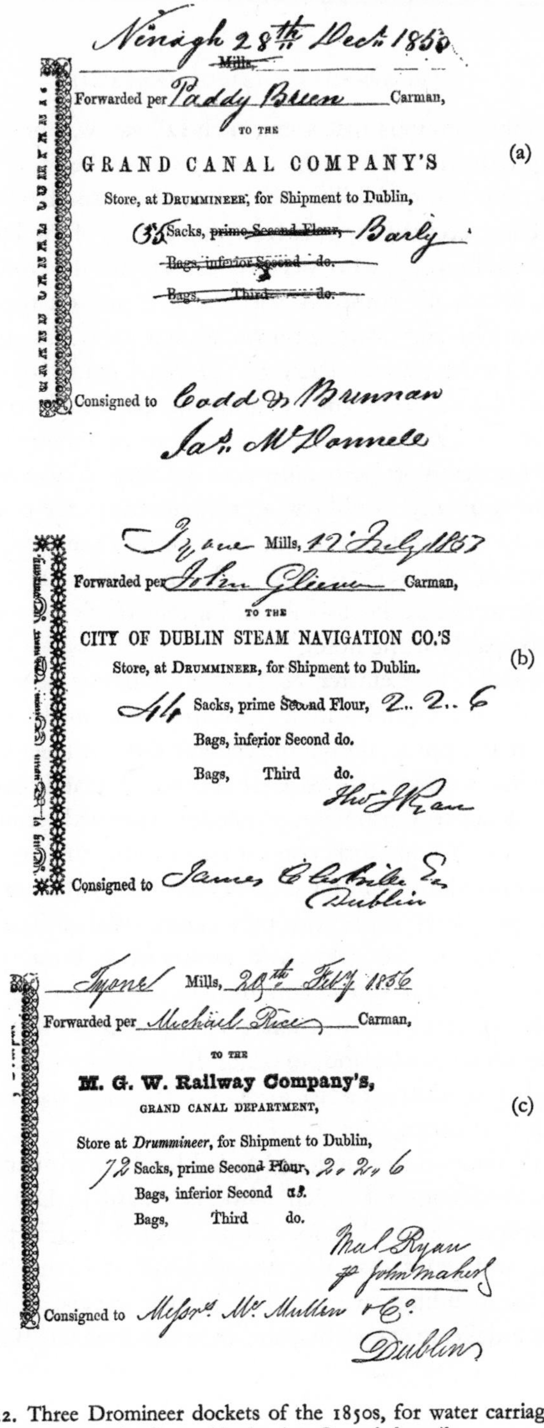

Nenagh 28th Decr 1850 ~~Mills~~,

Forwarded per Paddy Breen Carman,

TO THE

GRAND CANAL COMPANY'S

Store, at DRUMMINEER, for Shipment to Dublin,

35 Sacks, ~~prime Second Flour~~, Barly

~~Bags, inferior Second do.~~

~~Bags, Third do.~~

Consigned to Codd & Brennan

Jas. McDonnell

(a)

Tyone Mills, 12 July 1853

Forwarded per John Gleeson Carman,

TO THE

CITY OF DUBLIN STEAM NAVIGATION CO.'S

Store, at DRUMMINEER, for Shipment to Dublin.

46 Sacks, prime Second Flour, 2.. 2.. 6

Bags, inferior Second do.

Bags, Third do.

Thos J Ryan

Consigned to James Clibrile Esq Dublin

(b)

Tyone Mills, 20th Feby 1856

Forwarded per Michael Rice Carman,

TO THE

M. G. W. Railway Company's,

GRAND CANAL DEPARTMENT,

Store at *Drummineer*, for Shipment to Dublin,

72 Sacks, prime Second ~~Flour~~, 2.. 2.. 6

Bags, inferior Second do.

Bags, Third do.

Mal Ryan

pr John Maher

Consigned to Messrs. McMullen & Co.

Dublin

(c)

FIGURE 22. Three Dromineer dockets of the 1850s, for water carriage by the canal company, the Steam Navigation Co and the railway company

It became obvious that some such railway was going to be made, and the directors of the canal company therefore decided to look into the possibilities of a line along the banks of the canal. They received support from James Pim of the Dublin & Kingstown Railway, who was an enthusiast for the atmospheric system, which his company was about to use on the Dalkey extension.[3] In May 1844 John McMullen, who had succeeded Edward Lawson as secretary of the canal company in 1836, reported that he was having 'confidential communications with a number of gentlemen of the highest respectability' about a scheme for an atmospheric railway to Sallins and Monasterevan. The new company would pay an annual rent to the canal company of £250 in addition to one-tenth part of the receipts from any part of the railway alongside the canal. The Dublin terminus would be Portobello and a rent of £500 per annum would be paid for the hotel.

Meanwhile the Leinster & Munster Railway had failed to raise sufficient capital and no progress was made for some years. An attempt to revive the scheme did not meet with any success but a new route to Cashel (and ultimately to Cork), with branches to Carlow and Kilkenny, received strong backing from English interests connected with the carriage of mails and other goods to Dublin via Liverpool; they feared opposition from a proposed route through South Wales. The Cashel scheme, adopting the title Great Southern & Western, introduced a Bill in 1844 and a deputation of canal directors went to London to oppose it. An attempt was made by Lord Eliot, the Chief Secretary for Ireland, to bring the two sides together and, although they did agree to meet, no progress was made towards a settlement.

The deputation in London, headed by the chairman, Simon Foot, was in constant touch with the board in Dublin. The latter expressed a fear that opposition to the Bill might prejudice opinion and jeopardise the negotiations with the Treasury about the handing over of the branch canals, which had reached a delicate stage. In June 1844 the GS & WR Bill passed the Commons and, after a period of hesitation, the directors decided to continue the opposition in the Lords. In their petition they continued to press their own scheme for an atmospheric railway on the canal banks:

> Your Petitioners believe that certain Directors of the London & Birmingham Railway Company and their friends are very large proprietors of Railway Stock in England and they are interested in preventing any trials of the Atmospheric system, the success of which might cause a great dislocation in the value of Railway property generally.

The opposition failed and the Act authorising the GS & WR became law. The cost of the fight had been high; in addition to the expense of the deputation in London, a parliamentary solicitor sent in an account for over £1,000, although he eventually agreed to accept £850.

In December 1844 a deputation from the canal company met the directors of the GS & WR and offered the railway company the use of the canal banks to Sallins. Sir John Macneill, who, it will be remembered, had recently resigned as consultant engineer to the canal company to join the GS & WR, rejected the proposal as impractical. The canal company decided to pursue the matter and asked William Cubitt to make a survey. By this time a new threat had arisen to the main line of the canal. A new company, the Midland Great Western, had been formed and was negotiating with the Royal Canal Company with a view to purchasing the whole concern.[4] The banks of the Royal Canal would be used for a railway from Dublin to Mullingar and Longford and the promoters intended to have an extension to Athlone and Galway via Ballinasloe. The MGWR was being floated by a group who had broken away from the GS & WR, and the rivalry remained such as to cause the latter company to plan a connection from Portarlington to Tullamore and Athlone.[5] Thus it became clear that the prospects of the whole Grand Canal system were in jeopardy and William Cubitt was asked to consider the possibility of a line to Ballinasloe. He reported that he saw 'no Engineering difficulty whatever in laying down a double line of Railway suitable for locomotive power throughout the entire Line from Portobello to Ballinasloe'. His estimate for this scheme was one million pounds.

In March 1845 John McMullen, who had returned to London, informed the board that the promoters of the Dublin–Galway Bill had approached him with the suggestion that a rates agreement would be negotiated, giving the canal company preference in all heavy goods, if the latter would agree to withdraw all opposition to the Bill. The directors were furious with McMullen, 'and they feel the greatest astonishment that such a proposition should for a moment be listened to'. McMullen insisted that the only way to meet this new threat was to negotiate an agreement and he appealed to the board to allow him to proceed. The board was unanimous in refusing assent and Sir J. K. James was asked to go to London with power to use his discretion. The directors felt confident of the strength of their position because of the railway company's keenness to make them withdraw their opposition. At the same time a parliamentary agent was instructed to launch a company for the construction of a railway along the banks of the canal using William Cubitt's plans.

Eventually, in July 1845, the deputation in London reported that it had accepted an offer of £10,000, together with the sum of £900 owed to the parliamentary agent and an agreement to enter into negotiations about rates in return for withdrawing all opposition to the Bill. In September, however, the board advanced £1,000 to James Pim junior to enable him to lodge before Parliament plans of the railway along the banks of the canal, but in January, when he reported that he had done so and was considerably out of pocket, the board do not appear to have taken any further action in the matter.

In July of the following year, 1846, the GS & WR opened its line to Carlow with five trains a day and McMullen continued to press for negotiations so that 'some means may not yet be found whereby their now jarring interests may be reconciled,

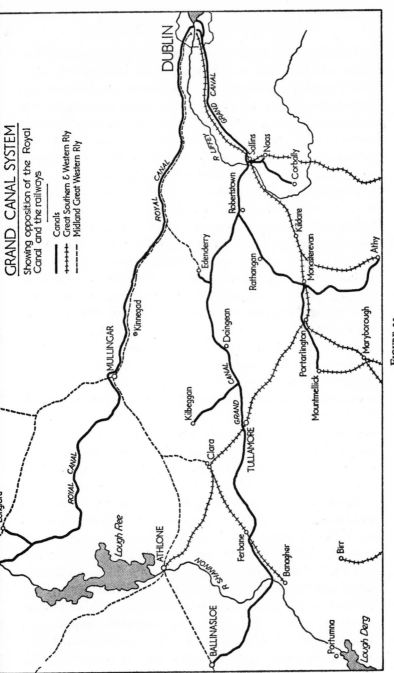

GRAND CANAL SYSTEM

Showing opposition of the Royal Canal and the railways

— Canals
+++ Great Southern & Western Rly
--- Midland Great Western Rly

FIGURE 23

and the foundation laid for a measure of future harmony and good understanding, if not co-operation'. In October 1847, following talks between the two companies, an agreement was sealed whereby the canal company agreed to terminate certain passenger services (as already shown in Chapter 6) and abandon parliamentary opposition to the Portarlington–Athlone extension, in return for a rates agreement giving the canal company preference in agricultural and heavy goods.

Lengthy negotiations were in progress all this time with the City of Dublin Steam Packet Company, which had absorbed the Shannon Steam Navigation Company. The existing agreement between the companies was due to expire in May 1843. This agreement gave the steam company special drawbacks on cargoes towed by its steamers which amounted to several hundred pounds each year and a bounty on passengers which cost the canal company about £400 per annum. The latter was considering terminating the steam company's monopoly on the river and perhaps introducing its own steam tugs. Trade on the Shannon was declining, with a corresponding decrease in the number of boats using the Grand Canal. The new Shannon commissioners agreed to lower tolls on the river if tolls on the canal for Shannon traffic were reduced. The canal company agreed to this and asked the traders to make a corresponding decrease in freights. Messrs Berry, one of the principal traders on the canal, accepted these proposals but the steam company said that they were 'objectionable and inquisitorial'.

Relations deteriorated, but it was obvious that the railways were going to present a grave threat to all water transport and so, in March 1845, a 'very lengthened and important conversation' took place between the two companies. No agreement was reached and, following an application from 96 manufacturers and merchants, the canal company decided to purchase a steam tug for the river. A boat was ordered from Thomas Wakefield Pim of Hull with a new type screw propeller at a cost of £3,580. She arrived in July 1846 and was named the *Shannon*. The City of Dublin SPC objected strongly to this interference with the Shannon trade and, finally, in 1850, decided to withdraw its boats from the Grand Canal and use the Royal Canal instead.

Legislation passed in 1845 clarified the position of canal companies carrying on their own canals.[6] In an attempt to fight railway competition the Grand Canal Company had decided in 1849 to enter this field and Kilbeggan and Naas were chosen for the experiment, the latter being included because Daly of Sallins, the only trader to Naas, had announced his intention of withdrawing the service which he was operating at a considerable loss. When the City of Dublin SPC withdrew from the Grand Canal, one year later, although the trading experiment had not proved very profitable, the canal company decided to try to take over the Shannon trade to avoid the transfer of the traffic to the Royal Canal. A bitter contest ensued and freights were cut on both sides until finally, in November 1852, an agreement was negotiated. The steam company surrendered the trade between Athlone and Limerick but retained the passenger traffic, which was operating in conjunction with the railways, and the Grand Canal Company agreed to divert as much traffic as possible to the SPC's cross-channel services. Meanwhile, Messrs Berry, the only other large carrier, realising that they would be unable to compete with the company's expanding carrying trade, offered to sell their whole establishment. Thomas Berry tried to include his appointment as agent at Shannon Harbour and Ballinasloe as one of the conditions of the sale, but the board refused to agree to this. Eventually, despite the intervention of Messrs Guinness, who had employed Berry's for over 30 years as their carriers and agents in the west of Ireland,[7] Thomas Berry had to accept the company's offer of £3,000. He retained the Guinness agency in Ballinasloe which had become an important distribution centre for the west; by this time the tonnage of porter carried on the Grand Canal had increased to about 2,500 tons a year.

Thus by the end of 1850 the company had taken over the

trade of the two principal carriers. The board decided to appoint a special committee to organise this new branch of the company's business and to improve the efficiency of the service. Agents were appointed at all the important places on the canal system and on the Shannon. At first they worked on a commission of 6d (2½p) per ton but later it was found necessary to pay them a fixed salary in addition to their commission. These agents were allowed to carry on business on their own account. For example, John Lawlor, the agent at Dromineer on Lough Derg in the 1850s, imported coal, herrings and other commodities, which he sold locally and he had dealings with Edward Murphy, the agent at Mountmellick over shipments of corn.[8]

Samuel Healy, who had replaced Andrew Bagot as inspector of trade and passage boats when the latter retired in 1847, had managed to purchase most of the City of Dublin SPC's boats and, with Berry's fleet and some new iron trade boats, the company had thirty-three craft in operation by the end of 1850. The Daly family of Sallins took over the haulage of most of the trade boats and regular hours of sailing were established. At the same time investigations were commenced with John Scott Russell about the possibility of introducing steam-powered trade boats on the canal. The *Shannon* with her screw propeller had proved very successful on the river and so, in August 1850, the board decided to order two screw trade boats. One of these, with a single screw, was commissioned from Robinson & Russell of Millwall for £500 and the second boat was ordered from Barrington's Dublin Dockyard Company at Ringsend to take a twin screw engine supplied by Inshaw's of Birmingham.

The two boats were ready early in 1851 and experiments supervised by Sir John Macneill were carried out to test their efficiency.[9] John McMullen, the secretary, reported that the boats achieved speeds of 2 to 3mph when fully laden, but he added, 'a considerable depth of water and the utmost available width of Canal, are indispensable where a loaded

Page 175   Former harbours in 1971: (*above*) Ballinasloe; (*below*) Portarlington on the Mountmellick Line. On the right is a lock-house, and in front of it a wall of the former lock

Page 176 The last barge, laden with Guinness's stout, leaves James's Street Harbour, Dublin, for Limerick, 1960

Boat is to be propelled and any moderate amount of expedition obtained'. Samuel Healy wrote a paper about these experiments which he delivered to the Institution of Civil Engineers in 1866.[10] He explained that they had found that there was a greater liability to damage with the double screw and an unnecessary multiplication of machinery without corresponding increased power. He added that these experiments, which involved placing the cargo in the steamer, where the space was limited by the engine machinery, had proved that it would be much more profitable to employ steam power in tugs, which could tow trains of boats. The laden steamers operating in the narrow confines of the canal were not a success and they were transferred to the Shannon but it was not until 1865–6 that three tugs were ordered from Grendons of Drogheda. Even these were only found practical on the long level.

The famine years and the fight against the railways made the 1840s a difficult time for the company financially. Dividends were suspended and matters came to a head in 1847. A loanholders' committee was formed, which presented a long report amounting to a strong condemnation of the directors, criticising the increasing expenditure of the company in the face of falling revenue. The committee angered the board by publishing a notice stating that it would be 'glad to receive information from Merchants and Traders and others interested in the carrying trade on the Canal with a view to remedying any abuses that exist'. Early in 1848, the board, unable to meet even the annual payments to the loanholders, recommended that the stock and loans should be consolidated. This was approved by the company and passed by Parliament in the same year.[11] The name was changed from the Company of the Undertakers of the Grand Canal to the Grand Canal Company, the capital was reduced to £665,938, the reserve fund was cut back to £10,000, the 6 per cent debentures were registered at £90, the 5 per cent at £75, the 4 per cent at £60 and the existing stock at £9. This enabled the company to start paying a small dividend and in the early 1850s, as the efforts of the carrying

L

trade committee began to show results, it was gradually increased to 1⅜ per cent in 1853.

In the 1848 reorganisation the number of directors was reduced from fifteen to not more than nine nor less than five, one-third of whom retired annually but were eligible for re-election. Two of the new directors were members of the loan-holders' committee, Dr Henry Hudson and John R. Corballis; the latter was elected deputy chairman, a position he held until 1869. Henry Fulton had also been a prominent member of the loanholders' committee, but he was not elected to the board. The other directors were John Barton, James Birch Kennedy, John McDonnell, George Pim and William Digges LaTouche; the latter was the son of a former chairman and had been a director since 1838; he now became chairman, a position he held until his death in 1882. Following this change in the board's constitution there was a much greater continuity of membership.

The new board had to cope with a serious breach in the bog embankment between Ticknevin lock (20th) and the Blundell aqueduct in February 1849. Apart from a small breach on the level above Ticknevin, near Derrymullen, which had closed the canal for two months in 1839, and the trouble with the Ballinasloe Canal, this was the first serious breach since the early days. The repairs had to be undertaken by the company's new engineer, Christopher Mulvany. It will be remembered that the company had tried to manage without appointing a resident engineer to replace John Stokes but, following Macneill's resignation, the board decided in 1847 to renew the appointment. Mulvany had been employed by the Board of Public Works before joining the canal company but, because the breach was the first test of his ability, he was hampered by the board, who were uncertain of his competence. Bernard Mullins, who had acted as an overseer when this section of canal was being constructed, was asked to inspect the breach and contract for the repairs. In the meantime Mulvany had constructed dams and laid a tramway along the north bank to enable the trade to continue.

Mullins was reluctant to undertake the work and Mulvany proceeded to erect a double range of piling across the opening, driven 9ft into the gravel below the bog. He employed over 1,000 men, but the board became impatient with the protracted closure of the canal. Mulvany insisted that the 'work altogether is conducted with a combined view to expedition, permanency, utility and economy' and refused to be hurried. Mullins was asked to inspect the progress and he added to Mulvany's difficulties by saying that the work was being carried out 'with a particularity much beyond our views'. Mullins's opinion of the danger of using piles has already been noted in connection with the Ballinasloe Line and he held that the work could have been achieved by using 'back-cutting of bog' as was done when the embankment was originally constructed. He did add, however, that Mulvany 'supports his views with ability and that he is undoubtedly a laborious and zealous officer, and with a little more experience, added to his respectable professional attainments, a valuable acquisition to the Company'. Mulvany had to cope with a breach in the Kilbeggan Line at the same time and, eventually, on 1 July, the canal was reopened, the combined cost in repairs and facilities to maintain the traffic at the two breaches amounting to £9,514.

In November 1850 the board received an offer 'from certain parties of unquestionable respectability connected with the Shipping Interests of the Port of Dublin' to take a lease of Ringsend basin and graving-docks. They had not proved profitable and had been rendered increasingly useless by improvements carried out to the port of Dublin by the Ballast Board.[12] In the 1840s the average number of boats entering the basin was about 600, although there was a temporary increase with famine relief ships in 1846–8. About 100 boats used the dry-docks each year and the total revenue from the whole concern amounted to about £1,000 per annum.[13] The directors now agreed to accept an annual payment of £600 and the terms of the lease were worked out. The canal company would retain the smallest of the three sea locks and the lessees would take over the rest of the concern with an undertaking to retain the rates and regulations in consultation with the canal company. The lease was negotiated for thirty years from 1 November 1851 and Wight Pike and Fred Barrington accepted the terms on behalf of the other interested parties. Barrington developed the dry-dock business and built many of the company's iron trade boats. In the 1870s the number of boats entering the basin increased to an average of 800 a year with over 100 boats using the dry-docks. In 1867 the Ballast Board was replaced by the Port and Docks Board and further improvements were carried out to the port over the next few years including extensive new deep water quays.[14] The Dublin Dockyard Company found it increasingly difficult to run the concern economically and in 1870 an attempt was made to surrender the lease, but the canal company refused to accept a surrender until its termination in 1881.

The canal company reverted to the old system of charging boats for the use of the dry-docks and allowing the owners of the boats to make their own arrangements for repairs. In 1913 the dry-docks were leased to William McMillan, who with William Alexander, his chief draughtsman, started the Ringsend Dockyard Company. The large dry-dock area was acquired by Heitons as a coalyard in 1918 and, when the Ringsend Dockyard Company went out of business in 1963, the two remaining dry-docks were taken over and filled in by the gas company. Over the years this company had gradually increased its holdings at Ringsend. It is amusing to note that in 1823 the Hibernian Turf Gas Company had offered to put a gas pipe into the company's house at Ringsend free of charge. The company accepted the offer but added, 'it is not probable that they will ever have any occasion to use Gas Light'. In 1833, however, an agreement was reached with the Gas Company to supply three lamps at James's Street and two at Portobello at an annual cost of £5 10s (£5.50) per lamp and subsequently gaslight was installed throughout the city premises.

Messrs Guinness had built a malt store at Ringsend, beside

the railway embankment, in 1866 and, because they undertook
to transport over 40,000 tons of export porter, malt, hops and
coal between the docks and James's Street every year, the canal
company agreed to charge them a nominal rent for the store.
After some years the canal company complained that the
promised tonnage was not being sent by water and Guinness's
tried to extract themselves from the agreement by substituting
a rent for the store. A rent of £600 was agreed, but in 1885,
when the new malt store was built at Bond Harbour, James's
Street, the Ringsend premises were surrendered, although they
continued to be rented on an annual basis at a reduced figure
until recent years.

To return to the company's position with the railway companies. The agreements were not proving very satisfactory,
being frequently violated by the railway companies. A deputation of canal directors waited upon the board of the GS & WR in
1849 to complain about these violations but they received little
consideration. The chairman of the railway company said that
they 'placed no value whatever upon the existing agreement,
and would be ready at any moment to cancel it, and asked could
the Deputation at once sanction them in destroying it'. The
agreement remained in force but the violations continued.

In July 1850 a joint meeting was held attended by the chair-
men of the GS & WR, the MGWR, the City of Dublin SPC and the
Grand Canal Company with William Dargan of the Steam Ship
Association in the chair. At this meeting the MGWR agreed to
the canal company's request for a 10 per cent differential, but
the GS & WR would not co-operate. Two months later, using a
small violation by the canal company as a pretext, the GS & WR
declared that it felt itself no longer bound by the 1847 agreement.

In 1852 negotiations commenced with the GS & WR with a
view to arranging a purchase of the whole canal undertaking.[15]
The railway company offered to pay £12,000 pa with an option
to purchase for £300,000. The Royal Canal had been bought
for £298,059 by the MGWR in 1845 and the Grand directors felt

that their concern was worth a great deal more. They suggested one £50 railway share for every £100 canal stock. At this stage the MGWR entered the negotiations, whereupon the GS & WR board agreed that 'the most vigorous measures' must be taken to prevent them acquiring the canal.[16] The GS & WR improved their offer to £13,200 per year or a purchase price of £330,000 but the canal directors accepted the MGWR offer of an exchange of shares. The rival company was furious and managed to have the Bill, authorising the takeover, thrown out by Parliament. It was then agreed that the MGWR would take a lease of the Grand Canal from 1 July 1853 for seven years or until parliamentary approval was obtained. An annual rent of £19,564 was arranged, providing the canal company shareholders with a dividend of $2\frac{1}{4}$ per cent which represented the amount they would hope to receive after the transfer of shares. The Grand Canal Company would continue to be responsible for the maintenance of the canal while the lease was in operation and the railway company would take over the carrying trade, tolls, rents and all other receipts such as fines and turnpike tolls.

The canal company directors reduced their meetings to one day a week and must have looked forward to the final winding up of the company, but the coup d'état of the MGWR had sparked off a bitter struggle between the railway giants, with the canal company a pawn in this battle.[17] The GS & WR promoted a Bill for the extension of the Portarlington–Tullamore line (which was nearly completed) to Athlone, invading MGWR territory. The latter replied with a Bill for a line from Streamstown to Tullamore, but neither received parliamentary approval. A Bill was then presented by the Grand Junction Railway Company, which invaded MGWR territory and had been promised financial backing by the GS & WR, but this was also thrown out after a severe and expensive contest. At this stage both sides agreed to negotiate and, when no agreement could be reached, it was announced in August 1854 that they would allow the matter to be settled by arbitration.

The question of the future of the Grand Canal became deeply involved in the struggle and a provisional agreement was reached in February 1855 that the two railway companies would divide the canal, the MGWR taking the main line to Ballinasloe and the Kilbeggan Line and the GS & WR acquiring the Barrow and Mountmellick Lines. The canal directors, alarmed by news of this deal, sought an assurance that the take-over would be carried through as promised and the MGWR replied that the matter would continue to be treated with 'the same good faith and integrity'.

On 13 September 1855 an extensive breach occurred in the bog embankment, west of the Blundell aqueduct, at the site of the earlier breaches. The canal company was responsible for maintenance and Mulvany began repairs as quickly as possible. Over 600ft of bank had been carried away on the north side and the south bank had slipped into the bed of the canal. Mulvany employed over 500 men at an average wage of 2s (10p) per day. He used two rows of piles set back about 25ft from the edge of the canal. The piles were 36ft long and he drove them in 10ft apart for a distance of 630ft and sheeted them with planks. William Dargan, who had been asked to undertake the repairs, refused, but he did agree to inspect Mulvany's work and supported his method of tackling it. The canal was re-opened on 11 January, but the four-month closure did not improve relations with the MGWR, who were finding that the canal was a poor financial investment.

In 1856 the Board of Trade turned down the proposal for the joint ownership of the canal and in the following year parliament authorised the GS & WR extension to Athlone on condition that it did not cross the Shannon and a MGWR line from Streamstown to Clara, not Tullamore as originally sought. The lease with the Grand Canal Company was due to expire in June 1860 and a Bill for the purchase of the canal by the two railway companies was presented to Parliament early in that year. In May William LaTouche, who had gone to London to follow the progress of the Bill, reported to the board in Dublin that the railway companies had decided to withdraw it on the grounds that the schedule of tolls proposed by Sir Richard Griffith was too low to afford an adequate return on the capital. The government had been under heavy pressure from the traders to maintain the low rates existing on the canal and an attempt to persuade Sir Richard Griffith to reconsider the question met with no success.

On 1 June 1860 the canal company received a short letter from the MGWR stating that the canal concerns would be handed back in one month: 'I am desired further to add', the letter continued, 'that our Board do not consider it incumbent upon them to make any renewed applications to Parliament for the purchase of the Grand Canal.' The canal company protested in the strongest possible terms about this breach of faith. The directors sought legal advice but they were advised that there was nothing they could do to enforce the agreement to purchase. Thus they had to accept that they still had a canal on their hands and that they once again had a responsibility to the shareholders to produce a dividend. They continued to do this with remarkable efficiency despite the network of railways which was growing around their system, and the canal company managed to hold its own for close on another century.

CHAPTER 9

The Struggle Continues

CONSCIOUS that it had dealt unfairly with the canal company, the MGWR negotiated a new agreement in July 1861 which gave differential rates ranging from 15 to 10 per cent. The railway company, which had built up a trade with steamers on the Shannon, agreed to confine these to Athlone and places north, leaving the river south of Athlone to the canal company; both concerns would continue to compete for the Athlone trade. Apart from some minor infringements this agreement remained in force until 1875. In that year the railway company sought a reduction in the differentials and insisted that goods from all places not directly on the canal must be excluded. The canal company, which had been trying to extend its trade beyond the confines of the system, refused to accept these modifications and the agreement was terminated. This had a much more serious effect on the canal company and, one year later, forced by 'the unmercantile opposition' of the railway company, which had lowered its freights to a point of little profit, the canal company accepted the terms. A new agreement was signed in March 1876 which, as it will be seen, was terminated by the canal company in 1889.

On the other front the canal company managed to come to terms with the GS & WR in 1863. Similar differentials were negotiated and this agreement remained in force until 1886, with some minor adjustments, usually to the advantage of the railway company. In 1886 the GS & WR suggested new terms which would deprive the canal company of the differential rate to many important stations and reduce it to 5 per cent to all the others. The canal company protested that these terms 'would practically extinguish any profit derivable from the Grand Canal trade'. Negotiations failed, the agreement was terminated and in the same year the GS & WR's new line from Clara to Banagher was completed, which further injured the company's trade.

Both sides now began to lower rates to attract traffic. The railway company made attractive offers to some of the canal's long-standing customers. Odlum's, millers in Portarlington, said that they had been offered a freight of 4s (20p) per ton with a railway siding to the mill. The freight by water was 5s 3d (26p) per ton and the board told Odlum's that it would not be possible to lower this. It was suggested that if they would be prepared to operate their own boats they would be offered a very low toll. Odlums agreed to this and eventually had three boats on the canal serving Portarlington and their other mills.

The rates war produced such a disparity in rates, which were still tied by the MGWR agreement, that in 1889 the board decided to terminate this agreement as well. In the following year the MGWR offered Guinness's Brewery a quotation of 10s (50p) per ton for dispatching porter to Ballinasloe. This presented a serious threat, because porter was rapidly becoming one of the most important commodities on the canal. The canal company was forced to lower the freight from 12s 6d (62½p) to 10s (50p) to retain the Ballinasloe trade.

The railway companies with their more extensive networks were able to quote very low rates to places served by both rail and water while maintaining higher rates elsewhere. In some investigations carried out by Guinness's Brewery in 1900 into comparative freight rates it was established that it would have cost 35 per cent more if the porter sent by water to places on the Shannon south of Shannon Harbour had been sent by rail. In the course of the same investigations the Grand Canal Company produced figures to show that the actual cost of conveying one ton of porter to Limerick was 8s 10d (44p) while the freight charged was 12s (60p) leaving a small margin of profit. It will be shown that the rates war developed to such ridiculous proportions that eventually new agreements were worked out, but first we must return to consider the other developments and activities of the company.

In 1863 the board decided to dispense with the William Street premises and move the company's administrative offices to James's Street harbour; £1,000 was authorised to carry out improvements and redecoration. Bond Harbour had been allowed to silt up badly by 1858 and the drawbridge needed replacing; the markets established by Sir James Bond had been abandoned in 1817. Colonel Hutchinson, who had inherited the harbour, was living in India but his agent obtained his permission to clean it out and the plans and estimates of the new drawbridge were sent to him for approval; this explains why this bridge was always known as 'Rupee Bridge'. Guinness's Brewery subsequently acquired this harbour and built their new malt store there in 1885, retaining some of the harbour; the remaining portion was filled in in recent years.

John McMullen, the secretary, had lived in the William Street house but by 1863 he had reached 'a very advanced time of life' and died just before the actual transfer took place. William Digby Cooke, his assistant, succeeded him and remained secretary until 1891, when he was forced to resign by defective eyesight; the board allowed him an annuity of £150 until his death in 1902. Samuel Healy, who had transferred to the MGWR during the years of the lease, rejoined the company in the newly created post of general traffic manager, which he held until his death in 1881. He was succeeded by his assistant, Thomas Wood Robinson, who was replaced in 1890 by James Kirkland. Kirkland had been employed by the Clyde Shipping Company in Dublin and the canal company offered him a salary of £400 a year. When Cooke had to retire, Kirkland became joint secretary and general manager, but he died suddenly in 1901. The board then promoted George Tough to general manager and Frederick Reid became secretary; when the latter retired in 1908, Tough took over the joint positions. Christopher Mulvany, the engineer, died in 1895 and was succeeded by his assistant, Francis Bergin. Bergin resigned in 1901 to become a consultant engineer and he was replaced by John Byrne, who was succeeded by Henry Wayte in 1907.

With a few exceptions most of the officers remained with the company all their working lives; some of them, if their health permitted, remained in office until they were very old men. Thomas Warham, the collector at James's Street, retired in his 91st year after serving the company for 46 years. His son, William, who had been helping him with his work, succeeded him and died in 1844 after 44 years service. William Warham junior then became collector but he resigned after 5 years to take over an uncle's business. The board always appointed a member of the same family to fill a vacancy if a suitable candidate was available.

The same system applied to the other employees of the company. Many of the locks were looked after by the same family through several generations. In the early days most of these families were Protestants, but this pattern gradually changed and the Mitchell family at the 30th lock, who have been looking after this lock since the very early years, are one of the last survivors of these families. Some of the families had their tragic stories. John Spain, the 26th lock-keeper, died of cholera in 1867. Thomas Spain at the nearby 24th lock was drowned in his lock a few years later and his brother, who succeeded him, was drowned in the same lock in 1890.

The free house and small garden offered security, but the wages were poor and the hours long. Some of the trade boats were issued with passes which entitled them to travel by night, and the lock-keeper was expected to be present when a boat was passing through his lock. The boats paid a small fee for the night pass, which was apportioned among the lock-keepers, but this did not amount to much. An amusing story is told of Thomas Murphy, lock-keeper at Lowtown in the early 1900s. He was asked by the chairman how long he had worked for the company and replied that he had worked for a hundred years, adding by way of explanation, 'fifty years by day and fifty by night'.

In the early days of the company the lock-keeper's wages ranged from 6s (Ir) to 8s 6d (Ir) per week, depending on the amount of work involved. During the famine years an increase of 1s 6d (7½p) was allowed and a further increase of 1s (5p) was granted in 1872 in response to an appeal that the 'present high prices of provisions, fuel and clothing made it difficult for them to exist'. In the 1870s overseers or bankrangers were paid about 12s 6d (62½p) per week, a foreman boatbuilder received about £1 10s (£1.50) and a sailmaker 18s (90p). A weekly allocation of 2s (10p) in winter and 1s (5p) in summer was made 'for the purpose of providing the requisite female assistance in washing and cleaning the Boardroom and offices'.

In 1873 the board weathered its first major strike for higher wages. The boatmen demanded an increase of 5s (25p) per week and the board replied with an offer of 2s (10p) to masters and 1s (5p) to crewmen. The men held out for eleven days but eventually agreed to return to work on the board's terms. In March 1890 the company had its first encounter with a trade union; the Amalgamated Trades' Society told the board that minimum hours and wages had been laid down for its members, who included some of the company's boatbuilders. A slight adjustment in hours was made but no increase in wages was granted. This was closely followed by a demand for increased wages from the drivers of the horses, the company having by this time taken over the haulage of the boats from the contractors. The board refused to comply with this demand and informed the public that traffic would be discontinued until new drivers were found. The boats were idle for six weeks and work was resumed when the company made a temporary arrangement to place the haulage out to contract. A new system of payment for the crews of the boats was introduced whereby they received a monthly bonus, based on the earnings of their boat. The employers were still operating from a position of strength, but it will be seen that this pattern gradually changed.

In 1877 a Boatmen's Benefit Society was set up to which the men subscribed 4d (1½p) each week, the company adding an equal amount per man. This money was used to help sick employees and, in the case of death, a payment was made to cover funeral expenses up to £3 with an additional £5 for the widow and children. There were quite a number of boatmen drowned over the years, the accidents usually occurring at night and more often than not owing to 'an excess of drink'. On these occasions the company usually made a payment of about £10 to the widow, but it was carefully stressed that this was an ex gratia payment and not an admission of liability. On one occasion a widow appealed through the courts but she was only awarded £15. Small sums were paid to employees in compensation for injuries received in the company's employment; a stableman received £10 for the loss of an arm. Claims for compensation were gradually increasing and in 1900 the company accepted a quotation from the Scottish Employers' Liability Company for insurance to cover accidents to employees at a rate of 5 per cent of the total wages bill of £29,000, but after five years the company decided to start its own insurance fund.

In the early years Willoughby Harcourt Carter had acted as the company's law agent, but in 1812 he was reported to have been 'out of the country for a considerable time' and William Duffield Rooke was appointed to succeed him. In 1893 Mr B. W. Rooke was informed that the board reserved the right to appoint whatever solicitor was considered the most suitable 'because of the varied nature of the business', and from that time Hayes & Sons became the company's solicitors.

The LaTouche family had always acted as the company's bankers but in 1870 the goodwill and business of their concern was transferred to the Munster Bank. This bank ceased payments in 1885 and went into liquidation, and the canal company, which lost £2,700, moved its business to the Royal Bank of Ireland.

It is interesting to trace the gradual emergence of the Circular Line through the city as we know it today in these closing years of the nineteenth century. In 1863 the board had received a proposal from the Metropolitan Junction Railway Company to purchase this stretch of the canal. The directors replied that 'the question of obliterating this portion of the Canal is very important indeed to the interests of this Company, and has occupied the anxious attention of the Directors'. They agreed to sell it for £80,000, the canal company retaining the ownership of one line of railway to the docks with a pipe conveying water to the basin at Ringsend, but nothing more was heard of this scheme. One by one the stretches of towpath between the city bridges were taken over and converted into roads. New housing schemes and buildings were erected, some of them involving leases from the company. In 1885 James Dillon asked for leave to erect an advertising board at Baggot Street Bridge at an annual rent of £25. Despite the objections of the local inhabitants, the company granted him permission and this was followed by requests for sites at the other bridges.

In 1862 the Electric and International Telegraph Company had been given permission to erect poles along parts of the canal at the nominal rent of 1s (5p) per mile, with the canal company receiving special rates for their own messages. The United Telephone Company continued to give the canal company special concessions in 1881, when James's Street was connected with the exchange and a line was laid to Ringsend.

It will be remembered that the canal company's agreement to supply Dublin Corporation with water was due to expire in 1865. The demands of the city were increasing rapidly and the quality of the supply from the canal was questionable. The corporation carried out investigations into the whole question of water supplies in the 1850s and negotiations were held with the canal company. At the same time the Rathmines Commissioners were contemplating the possibility of a supply from the canal. They obtained the opinion of an expert, Thomas Hawksley, who reported:

The waters of the Canals, as proved by analysis are of a good wholesome quality, and when taken from a proper distance from the city, and after being subject to the process of filtration, will be unobjectionable waters for domestic use, quite colourless, and of but a moderate degree of hardness.[1]

Acting on this advice, the Rathmines Commissioners reached agreement with the canal company in 1861 to obtain a supply from above the 8th lock, where they proposed constructing filterbeds. The canal company would receive 12½ per cent of a 6d (2½p) rate for each house supplied, producing an income of about £450 per annum.

Dublin Corporation decided to abandon the city basins and build a reservoir at 5th lock, and the canal company agreed to pay one-third of the cost, its share amounting to about £2,000. It was subsequently found necessary to add filter beds at an additional cost of £4,000. It was the intention of the corporation to use this supply for the brewers, distillers and other manufacturers in the city, with an estimated consumption of 4,000,000 gallons per day. The supply would be controlled by meters on the consumers' premises, with a complicated scale of charges, decreasing in proportion to the quantity used, producing an annual income for the canal company of about £1,000. In the meantime the corporation had constructed a reservoir at Roundwood in County Wicklow, supplied by the Vartry River, for domestic consumers.[2] The supply to the city's basin at James's Street was terminated on 24 June 1869 and Portobello basin was discontinued in the following year. These supplies had been producing an annual income of about £2,400 for the canal company, but a reserve fund had been set up to meet the loss of income. In addition the canal company had a number of agreements with firms to provide a water supply direct from the canal. The GS & WR paid £136 per annum and the Dublin & Wicklow Railway Company drew a supply from a small reservoir at the 3rd lock on the Circular Line. The Gas Company, the Dublin United Tramway Company, Bewley's sugar refinery and Boland's mills all drew supplies direct from

Ringsend basin. Most of the firms gradually changed over to the mains supply but some supplies are still obtained, including one from Portobello to the artificial ponds in St Stephen's Green, negotiated by Sir A. E. Guinness in 1897 at an annual rent of £50.

Rathmines Commissioners transferred to their own supply from the River Dodder at Bohernabreena in 1893 and the corporation acquired their filter beds. In that year the canal company's agreement with the corporation was renewed for thirty years, it being agreed that the company should receive half the gross receipts with a minimum price of 1½d per 1,000 gallons, the corporation being responsible for maintaining the works. In 1923 Mr Moynihan, the Deputy City Engineer, giving evidence before the Inland Waterways Commission, said that 500 to 600 million gallons of water per year were being drawn from the canal.[3] He pointed out that the canal water was particularly suitable for brewing and Guinness's Brewery, the principal consumers, did not wish to change to mains water; he added that the brewery carried out a daily analysis of the water to ensure that the quality was being maintained. He complained that the cost of maintaining the filter beds had greatly increased with the introduction of motor boats in 1911, which churned up the mud. In 1924, when the agreement came up for renewal, the corporation reluctantly agreed to raise the minimum price to 1¾d per 1,000 gallons but the canal company refused to give any undertaking about the quality of the water. The filter beds at the 8th lock are still used today and another pipe passes from there through the 5th lock works into the city.

The company's trade on the Shannon continued to expand. In the 1860s three new steamers joined the fleet, the *Dublin*, the *Limerick* and the *Athlone*. In 1868, the *Ballymurtagh* was purchased from the Wicklow Copper Mining Company to replace the *Shannon*, which was sold for £174. In the 1890s the *Portumna*, *Killaloe* and *Tullamore* were purchased and, in 1902, the *Carrick* (see Appendix 3). The Shannon Commissioners tried to increase their tolls in 1882 but the canal company resisted

M

this, saying that it would not be possible to increase the freight rates to meet the additional expense of £400 a year because of railway competition. In the face of a threat to withdraw the trade, the commissioners restored the old rates.

Mention has been made of the efforts of C. W. Williams and Jasper Rogers to utilise some of the large quantities of turf available in the midlands. Hand-won turf had always been one of the principal commodities carried on the canal. In the early part of the nineteenth century over 30,000 tons were carried to the city each year and this rose to over 40,000 tons in the 1830s. The company attached sufficient importance to the trade to advance loans to the turf cutters in the difficult days of the first half of the century, which were always repaid dutifully. Reductions in the price of coal gradually reduced the demand for turf, but it still remained the staple fuel of the poorer people, being sold by the sod, two or three sods for 1d.

In addition to this hand-won turf there were various attempts to develop peat industries.[4] In 1860 Charles Hodgson set up works at Derrylea, near Monasterevan, where he air-dried powdered turf and pressed it into briquettes.[5] The weekly output was about 180 tons which were transported by works railway to the canal at the 24th lock near Monasterevan and thence by boat to Portobello where stores were leased from the company. He was allowed a special toll of 1d per ton per mile, but the high cost of manufacture made it difficult to operate economically and in 1867 it was reported that his Patent Peat Company had collapsed and the sheriff had seized the plant and machinery.

Another venture was a peat litter factory at Ummeras near Rathangan set up by General Maquay in 1885. It continued to operate under different owners until it was accidentally burnt down in 1940. In addition to peat litter, other turf products were tried there; firelighters were made by soaking hard turf in an inflammable liquid and peat board was also produced, but this latter experiment proved a costly failure. A peat litter factory was operated from 1890 in the old mill premises at the

2nd lock, Inchicore, by Norman Palmer. When it was destroyed by fire in 1905, Palmer moved his operations to Drumcooley near Edenderry, sending the finished product to the city by water instead of importing the raw material as before. Palmer's factory was acquired by the Ummeras Peat Company in 1920 and, when the Ummeras factory was destroyed, production was concentrated at Drumcooley until the company ceased to operate after the 1939–45 war. Another peat works was operated by David Sherlock at Rahan from the 1890s until 1914.[6]

In the early 1900s many experiments were tried in artificial methods of drying turf. One of these, the 'Ekenberg wet carbonising process' was adopted by the Leinster Carbonising Company.[7] They obtained a lease of Colonel Dopping's peat moss litter factory at Turraun on Pollagh bog in 1910. After experiments had been carried out, it was eventually decided that all attempts to eject water forcibly from turf were unsatisfactory and the simple method of air drying was the most economic. Boats used the Lough Boora feeder canal to approach close to the factory, but in 1936 the works were taken over by the Turf Development Board and extensive operations in the area caused so much peat slurry to be carried down the feeder into the main canal that the supply had to be discontinued.

Another attempt to utilise turf was the Peat Fuel Company's briquette factory at Lullymore, near Robertstown, which went into production in 1934. It was hoped to produce 50,000 tons of briquettes each year but the firm ran into technical and financial difficulties and went into liquidation in 1939. It was also taken over by the Turf Development Board; this body had been set up by the government in 1934 to try to co-ordinate efforts to utilise turf. It became responsible for organising the shipment of large quantities of turf to the city to counteract the fuel shortage during World War II. Between 1941 and 1945 over 200,000 tons of turf and briquettes were carried by canal to the city.[8]

The Central Ireland Electric Power Company had been authorised in 1908 to commence operations to produce electricity using turf as fuel and a lease of land at Derrymullen, near Robertstown, was obtained in the following year.[9] Methods of harvesting turf were not sufficiently developed at this time and it was not until 1947 that the project was put into operation by the Electricity Supply Board. An agreement was negotiated with the canal company to obtain a supply of water from the canal for the cooling tower. The ESB agreed to pay an annual rent of £500 for twenty-five years and accepted responsibility for maintaining the water level for the navigation. In order to ensure this, the ESB took over a system of pumping water to the summit level from the River Liffey, which had been installed by the company some years earlier, paying the canal company £10,000 for the plant. The Turf Development Board, which had been reconstituted as Bord na Mona in 1946, set up extensive schemes to produce turf for the power station but this was all conveyed by specially laid light railways and the tonnage of turf carried by water continued to fall until, by the 1950s, it was amost non-existent.

The years of comparative peace with the railway companies in the 1860s and 1870s enabled the canal company to settle down to a period of steady growth with an average net surplus of about £20,000, producing an average dividend of 3 per cent. The tonnage carried on the canal rose to a peak of 379,047 tons in 1875, but thereafter it began to fall, as the following table illustrates:[10]

Year	Co's Boats tons	Bye-Traders tons	Total tons
1875	88,836	290,211	379,047
1878	98,983	227,454	326,437
1885	129,246	113,095	242,341

Year	Tolls	Profit per ton		Net Revenue	Dividend
	£	£ s d		£	per cent
1875	18,242	2 3¾		20,450	3
1878	16,857	2 1½		18,984	2⅝
1885	8,069	1 10		12,856	1¹¹⁄₁₆

There are several factors other than the railways which explain this decline. The late 1870s and early 1880s were years of general depression in trade and poor harvests and included some exceptionally severe winters which interfered with the canal trade. Guinness's Brewery were now using their own boats on the River Liffey to convey their export porter to the docks and this, coupled with the ending of the traffic in materials used in the construction of the railways, accounted for nearly 100,000 tons. The quantity of building materials carried by water had also declined. There had been an extensive trade in bricks from the Pollagh and Tullamore areas, amounting to 40,000 tons in the 1840s, but increased labour costs brought about the introduction of a larger type of brick, which was produced nearer Dublin, and the increase in the use of cement finally killed the trade in the early 1900s.

An increase in the tonnage carried in the company's boats and a corresponding decrease in bye-trader traffic was largely the result of the Barrow Navigation Company ceasing to trade north of Athy in 1878. The Grand Canal Company took over this trade amounting to about 21,000 tons a year. The Barrow company was in financial difficulties and had offered to sell its concern to the Grand Canal Company for £54,000, but the latter's offer of £48,000 was rejected and instead the decision was made to withdraw the north of Athy trade.

The shareholders had become apprehensive about the declining profits of the company and in 1886 J. G. V. Porter, a shareholder, who had been a constant source of annoyance to the board, managed to gather enough support to form a shareholders' committee. He used his newspaper, *Ireland's Gazette*, to wage war on the board and produced statistics to show the decline in the value of canal stock, which had fallen from £66 in 1878 to £33 in 1884.[11] The board refused to have any dealings with the committee. Brindley Hone, the chairman, told them, 'My Board so long as they remain in office and enjoy the confidence of the majority of the Proprietors hold themselves solely responsible for the management of the business of the

Company.' There was the usual interchange of correspondence and publication of accusations and statistics.[12]

The deterioration in the company's affairs was further aggravated by the termination of the GS & WR agreement in 1886 and the pressure of the shareholders' committee increased. Porter, the chairman, asked for facilities for the committee to visit the stations along the canal accompanied by one of the company's officers. The board agreed to allow the traffic manager to accompany them for a maximum of two days but added that it deprecated 'the perpetual and harassing attacks' of the committee and offered to resign at the next meeting if that was the wish of the majority of the shareholders.

The battle was continued in the newspapers and at the half-yearly meeting in February 1889 the directors replied in detail to some of the suggestions which had been put forward by the committee. These suggestions included the reduction in the number of the company's officers and the reintroduction of steam power on the canal, which were both rejected by the board as impractical. At that meeting W. F. deV. Kane, who had been a prominent member of the shareholders' committee, was elected to the board; he became a very active member, constantly laying reports and recommendations before his colleagues.

At a special meeting in October a resolution, increasing the number of directors from six to the maximum of nine, was passed and three more of the shareholders' committee were elected. Hone resigned from the chair, Kane became chairman and a sub-committee was appointed to study the situation. Some reductions in staff were made and there was a general tightening up in financial control. Kevans & Son, chartered accountants, commented that the 'bookkeeping of the Company requires to be thoroughly overhauled and modernised'. E. J. Lloyd, from the Warwick & Birmingham Canal Company, was invited to undertake an inquiry and some of his recommendations were implemented. At his suggestion all departments were amalgamated under two heads, engineering and

Grand Canal Company.

AGENT'S OFFICE,

JAMES'S STREET HARBOUR,

Dublin, *3 9* 189*7*

To Agent *Dromineer*

GOODS AMISSING.

Portumna Agent reports being
deficient *1 bx soap malone*
1 bale paper malony.
from *Per Str Duffy or from Dublin*
handed us on *28th* inst.

Have you any trace? If overlanded with you
please send _____ to *Portumna*
by first boat, advising me.

Yours truly,

J. R. READ,

Agent.

FIGURE 24. Goods amissing

traffic, each controlled by a committee of directors, and the proceedings of these committees, including weekly accounts, were read and confirmed by the full board. Lloyd criticised the general maintenance of the canal and suggested that the duties of the bankrangers should be laid down more clearly, with their districts properly defined, and that the company should take over the upkeep of the banks and trackways from the various contractors when their contracts expired.

James McCann, who had been instrumental in bringing about the enlargement of the board and who was one of the largest holders of stock, was elected to the board in 1891 and became chairman in the following year. He was responsible for continuing the reforms. One of his first actions was to force a conclusion to the long protracted negotiations with the Barrow Navigation Company. The condition of the Barrow had become so bad that the trade was seriously hindered and McCann threatened to withdraw the company's boats. Trade on the river had reached a very low ebb and the Carlow town commissioners complained of a 'total cessation of trade' south of Carlow. The Barrow company agreed to accept an offer of £30,000, with an additional £2,500 for plant and equipment, which it will be remembered was a great deal less than the offer they had rejected some years earlier. The Grand Canal Act 1894 authorised the purchase and permitted the Grand Canal Company to raise the necessary capital, bringing the authorised capital to £765,900; the stock was reorganised into £10 shares, 50 per cent of which were preference with an annual dividend of 3 per cent.[13]

The purchase of the Barrow company added over 40 miles of navigable river with 23 locks and side canals to the Grand Canal system.[14] The navigation was subject to the usual difficulties of river navigations, such as fluctuations in level, heavy currents in time of flood and silting in the side canals, and the Grand Canal Company did nothing to tackle the major problems of improving the waterway. The takeover also brought about a new phase in the war of rates with the GS & WR. The chairman of the Barrow company had been Mr Colville, who was also chairman of the railway company and he had been able to protect the interests of the navigation. Now, however, the canal company found that the GS & WR was endeavouring to take over the trade of the Barrow valley. They replied by attacking the railway's trade to places not directly on the canal system. For example, on the Shannon Navigation, attempts were made to secure the coal trade in Nenagh by providing road transport from the company's station at Dromineer on Lough Derg. The situation gradually worsened until both companies were operating some of their services without any profit and even the railway company, with its more extensive network, was ready to negotiate. Finally, in 1900, after lengthy talks, the canal company agreed to give up trading in places not directly served by water (principally trade in coal) in return for an annual payment of about £4,000, which was based on a fixed percentage of the profit sacrificed by surrendering this trade. A schedule of rates was agreed which could not be altered without consultation, but George Tough, giving evidence before the Royal Commission on Canals and Inland Waterways in 1906, explained that the trading public did not suffer as a result of this schedule because the prices were based on the low rates produced by the war of rates.[15]

An agreement had been negotiated with the MGWR in 1894 which allowed the canal company differential rates, ranging from 5 to 10 per cent, to certain specified places. Before James McCann died in 1904, he had succeeded in placing the canal company in a much sounder financial position, as shown overleaf.[16]

By 1905 the company was operating a fleet of over 70 trade boats with 4 tugs on the canal and 5 large vessels on the Shannon, and the shareholders were able to look forward to a steady dividend of 4 per cent.

Year	Co's Boats tons	Bye-traders tons	Total tons
1888			228,545
1898	221,985	87,303	309,288
1905	192,551	99,373	291,924

Year	Revenue £	Expenditure £	Net Surplus £	Ordinary Dividend per cent
1888	62,495	49,442	13,053	$1\frac{13}{16}$
1898	89,037	65,424	23,613	4
1905	90,782	67,201	23,581	4

CHAPTER 10

The Final Years

IT will be remembered that steam tugs had been introduced on the long level in 1865. It was found, however, that this system caused such lengthy delays, while the boats assembled to form trains for the tugs, that horse haulage was reintroduced in 1872. Pressed by the shareholders' committee to use steam power to increase the speed of the trade boats, the board decided to try two-horse haulage in 1889. This produced very little increase in speed and in 1891 single-horse haulage and steam tugs on the long level were restored. At the same time some correspondence was carried on with Priestman's of Hull about their new oil engine and James McCann visited Newry 'to inspect William Barcroft's invention of large, partially submerged propellers'. The Priestman engine was not tried but Barcroft did operate a boat on the canal for some time, although no attempt was made to convert other boats.

In 1910 Henry Wayte, the company's engineer, recommended trying an oil engine, and a four-cylinder Scott Sterling engine was purchased for £69. This engine was installed in May of that year but it was not a success. In the following year the board allowed Wayte to become the Irish agent for Bolinder engines and four of these were fitted. A trial trip was carried out in July 1911 and was reported to be 'very satisfactory'. More engines were ordered and by 1914 twenty-eight boats had been converted.

The system of numbering the boats* needs some explana-

* Always referred to as 'canal boats' not 'barges'.

tion. Prior to 1870 all boats, when they were registered, were given consecutive numbers. In that year the numbers passed 1,000 and it was decided to start a new series, the company's new boats being numbered commencing with No 1 and the bye-traders' boats (known as hack boats) with 1B. The numbers had not reached 100 in the new series when the prefix M was introduced to denote the company's boats in which engines had been installed, commencing with 1M. The bye-traders continued to use the prefix B and the company's maintenance boats, usually old trade boats, were given the prefix E. The government subsidised the building of twenty-nine boats during World War II to cope with the transport of turf to the city, and these were denoted by the letter G. These boats, built of unseasoned timber without engines, were not intended to remain long in service and some of them were broken up by the company after the war; others, bought by bye-traders, were not broken up for some years.[1]

The first thirty M boats were all converted horse boats and it was not until 1925 that 31M was built by the Ringsend Dockyard Company at a cost of £1,100. Between 1925 and 1939, forty-eight boats were built for the company, most of them by the Dublin Dockyard Company and Vickers (Ireland) Limited (subsequently the Liffey Dockyard Company), the rest by the Ringsend company. The B boats eventually numbered up to 133B but some of these were purchased from the company and renumbered. Most of the bye-traders followed the company's lead and converted to engines, the last new boat, 113B, being built for James Hughes of Athy in 1937 by the Ringsend Dockyard Company.

In 1938 the Ringsend company won the contract to build a new motor boat for the company's Shannon trade; she was called the *St James* and cost £3,240. Two more large motor boats, the *Avon King* and the *Avon Queen* were purchased from the River Severn in 1946 at a combined cost of £5,000 and were renamed the *St Patrick* and the *St Brigid*. The two locks leading out into the river from Shannon Harbour, which it will be remembered had been originally built to a larger size, had to be further enlarged to permit these boats to come up to the harbour to tranship.

In the last fifty years of the company there were few changes on the board: Frank Dillon, H. S. Sankey, the Rt Hon Laurence Waldron, Edmund Williams, William Odlum, the Rt Hon James MacMahon, Matthew Minch and John McCann all served long tenures. Laurence Waldron was chairman from 1906 until his death in 1924 and John McCann, son of James McCann, then took over the chair until the company was amalgamated with Coras Iompair Eireann in 1950. George Tough, the joint secretary and general manager, was succeeded by Thomas Delaney as secretary in 1913. When Tough retired in 1914, Henry Phillips became traffic manager. He had joined the company in 1891 as a clerk with £75 pa and in 1919 he was promoted to general manager with £360 pa. As already mentioned he was very interested in the history of the company and wrote articles for several journals.[2] He lived in the general manager's house at James's Street Harbour until his death in 1937 when his assistant John Hall Scott became general manager. Thomas Delaney retired in 1948 after fifty-six years service with the company and John Scott took over the combined positions until the amalgamation. Henry Wayte, the engineer, resigned in 1919 and was replaced by Herbert Day, who remained the company's engineer until 1931 when Charles Calwell succeeded him.

These were years of increasing labour unrest. In 1908 a short strike among the boatmen had been quickly broken but in September 1911 the company had its first major clash with the unions. The trouble was not over increased wages or shorter working hours, but involved the dismissal of some of the 'bulkers' at James's Street. The 'bulkers', who loaded and unloaded the boats, refused to handle timber from a merchant whose men were on strike. The canal company dismissed the bulkers and the rest of the men struck in sympathy. Negotiations for a return to work were held up by the union, which was trying to define the men's rights in the issue. The directors insisted that it was not practical that the men should be allowed to dictate their duties or question the right of the company to dismiss men; a document was drawn up to this effect which the men were asked to sign. The men refused to do so and the directors said that they would not reinstate the bulkers. The latter prevented a boat loaded by clerical staff from leaving the harbour but, ultimately, the men signed and returned to work on 25 October and the board agreed that in future regular bulkers would be employed at a fixed rate per ton.

In 1913 the ITGWU had its showdown with the employers which resulted in the famous lockout. Arnold Wright in his account of the strike, *Disturbed Dublin*, published in 1914, states that some of the canal company employees came out on strike at the end of September over the handling of 'tainted goods' and that traffic was resumed in early December. This is confirmed in the records of the company, but it is difficult to establish the extent of the stoppage. The monthly accounts of the boatmen's and drivers' wages continued but at a reduced level and on 25 November it was reported that the ITGWU had made an unsuccessful attempt to stop the trade on the Shannon. In their half-yearly report for this period the directors explained that the revenue of the company showed a decrease of £11,011 over the corresponding period in the previous year, 'due almost entirely, directly or indirectly to the strike'. A ballad sung by the boatmen was written to commemorate the strike:

> Oh James's Street did echo to Larkin's bugle call
> And for the rights of Irishmen, we rallied one and all,
> Those tyrants 'Tough' and 'Allen' we left in sad dismay,
> When they closed the gates behind us as we struck for higher
>   pay . . . etc[3]

Wages were supplemented by war bonuses during World War I and, on 1 July 1917, the Board of Trade assumed financial responsibility for maintaining the canal and supplementing the wages. A bonus of 6s (30p) was granted to all the boatmen and labourers bringing the average weekly wage to £1 5s. (£1.25). The subsidy, awarded by the government, amounted to about £40,000 each year.

The directors were still adopting an attitude of ignoring the unions. Applications for higher wages were passed on to the control board but a letter in connection with the dismissal of an employee was marked 'not to be recognized in any way'. War bonuses were steadily increased and in the years immediately after the war demands continued for higher wages and shorter hours. Henry Phillips, the general manager, warned the board that the position was serious. The company would not be able to meet the increased wages bill when government support was withdrawn, and traffic was being lost because it could not be handled in the shorter working hours. A meeting took place between the transport unions, the company and the men, in the presence of a negotiator, and an agreement was worked out, but the men refused to accept it and went on strike in defiance of the unions in December 1919. The men wanted to be paid by the hour instead of by the ton for overtime in loading and discharging boats, but they finally agreed to return to work on 5 February at an increased rate per ton. This was followed in March by another strike which lasted two weeks over the dismissal of some men at the Limerick station.

The directors appealed to the Board of Trade to continue to give the company financial support and it was agreed to extend the subsidy until 31 August 1920. The company was authorised to increase its freights and tolls up to a maximum of 150 per cent to help meet the increased costs. Demands from the unions continued, but the company was unable to meet them and by the end of 1921 a decrease in trade on the canal forced the company to lay off some men and reduce wages, which were still being augmented by war bonuses. This action brought an outcry from the unions but the company insisted that it had no alternative and on 27 January 1922 the men came out on strike. After a month of negotiation a return to work was arranged on a temporary settlement, which allowed some reductions, pending the setting up of a commission of inquiry. It was subsequently decided by the new Free State government to extend this inquiry to cover all the waterways and the commission began to take evidence on 16 January 1923, being the first commission undertaken by the new government.

The following table illustrates the position of the company before, during and after the war years:[4]

Year	Co's Boats tons	Bye-traders tons	Total tons
1910	174,846	116,056	290,902
1912	174,551	134,300	308,850
1915	145,764	113,384	259,148
1920	107,389	119,259	226,648

Year	Revenue £	Expenditure £	Net Surplus £	Ordinary Dividend per cent
1901	88,200	63,666	24,543	4
1912	89,877	68,671	21,206	4
1915	83,822	59,593	24,229	3
1920	135,565*	117,109	18,456	3

It will be noticed that the proportion of bye-trader traffic had gradually increased again and actually exceeded the tonnage carried by the company in 1920.

Another factor that hampered the company in this period was a serious breach in the north bank of the canal near the Blundell aqueduct, at the site of the 1855, 1800 and 1797 breaches. On 11 January 1916 300yd of bank were carried away and Wayte estimated that it would take twelve weeks and cost about £6,000 to carry out the repairs. He erected dams to try to keep the trade moving and to help bring clay to the site, estimating that 25,000 tons would be needed. The breach was described in detail in the *Leinster Leader*:

> The scene of the canal burst at Edenderry has been visited by thousands of people during the past week, and visitors from all parts of the country have motored there to inspect the remark-

* Including government subsidy of £40,357.

able sight. They all of them admit that no description, however graphic, could have prepared them for what they saw—the havoc wrought by the muddy rushing water, the enormous force that must have pressed it outwards, the utter impotence of the protecting line to resist the pressure and the great cataclysm that resulted. . . . Again the breach took place on exactly the same spot as the great breach of sixty years ago. You can see the great wooden piles that had been sunk that time. They are about 15ft away from the edge of the canal and are still fresh and strong looking. Deeply embedded in the ground, they must have been capable of resisting enormous pressure. Yet here they lie tossed here and there like so many matches, their impotence being the most illuminating record of the mighty power that swept them away.[5]

The newspaper reported that 'an English gentleman' had suggested that the breach had been caused by an earthquake, which was recorded in England on that day, but this is very unlikely from the evidence. Gordon Thomas, engineer to the Grand Junction and Regent's Canals, was asked to come over to confer with Wayte about the cause of the breach. He attributed the immediate cause to the 'boisterous weather' and 'heavy rainfall' which had raised the water level and imposed an additional strain on the already weakened bank:

The action of nature has for some years past been active in preparing the several constituent works for their collapse, there is an apparent lack of the necessary works of reparation to the ravages of time and weather, and the erosion inseparable from the strenuous working of the Navigation resulting in excessive seepage and leakage; the main lateral and cross drains being in a more or less blocked state, the water penetrated to the bed of the old slip, this too in a great measure contributed to the wreck of the structure. . . . The expense of maintaining a Canal increases with the number of propelled boats navigating upon it.

Wayte decided to use three rows of new piles, backed and filled in with bog material and clay. The weather was very severe, with hail and snow, and Wayte reported that the water backed up on the long level and he had to run it off by a foot to prevent it flooding over the dam. Two weeks later, early in

N

February, he reported that the weather was 'simply abominable —gales and snow'. The men were exhausted and he made Sunday working optional; they worked from 7.30am to 5.30pm, with an hour's break for dinner, and were paid £1 5s (£1.25) per week. The piles were gradually driven in and, early in March, he said that sixty of them were now in position but 'light snow fell unceasingly on Friday; there was a bad blizzard all Saturday and only half the men turned in'. By the end of March the work was nearly completed and the board praised Wayte for his efforts. 'The hardships we have endured', he replied, 'have to a great extent been repaid by the welcome praise and comments by the several Directors.' The water was admitted early in April and, in his eleventh weekly report, Wayte was able to say that the work had been completed within the estimated time and cost. Since then there has been one serious breach on the canal, though not on this level. It occurred near Derries Bridge on Pollagh bog, west of Tullamore, in January 1954 and took four months to repair.

During the Easter Week rising in 1916 all traffic near the city was halted for about ten days. Henry Phillips reported:

> The Insurrectionists being in possession of the Distillery outside the Harbour, shots were exchanged with Military in Messrs Guinness's Hop store at the other end of the Harbour. Barricades were placed by the Military outside the Harbour in two positions. Owing to the shortage of provisions I distributed Flour, Bacon and Sugar to Company's Staff and employees at cost price. About three hundred people were thus spared the pinch of hunger.

A little damage was reported to canal works for which the company was eventually awarded nearly £50 compensation but no allowance was made for the loss of revenue while the trade was stopped. A boat belonging to the Irish Paper Mills was sunk in one of the city locks but no other boats were damaged.

The Civil War in 1922 had a much greater effect on the canal although traffic continued throughout the hostilities. The board was unable to meet for two weeks 'owing to Civil

Commotion in the City' and the general manager reported incidents in various parts of the country. The store at Banagher was taken over by the Irregulars, who raided boats and stored the contents there, issuing it out to people by permit. The main Limerick road bridge near Monasterevan was blown up and attempts were made to breach the Ballinasloe Line. The company's store at Rahan was commandeered by the IRA for dances. On the Shannon, Dromineer store was burnt down and damage was reported to the Limerick–Killaloe Canal. There were frequent attacks on the trade boats and these raids, as many as four a week, continued into 1923. The boatmen refused to allow armed guards to accompany the boats because they feared that this would lead to clashes endangering their lives. One boat, which did carry an armed guard, was ambushed by the IRA on the Shannon near Clonmacnoise. The company's records state that 12 May 1923 was the day 'on which it is held that the country ceased to be in a condition of war', but the raids on the boats continued for some time.

The Canals and Inland Waterways Commission issued its report in July 1923.[6] A great deal of evidence had been heard from traders about the restrictions in the channel caused by accumulations of mud and weeds and the insufficiency of depth in dry seasons, particularly on the Barrow Navigation. The control of weed had always been a problem and over the years many different methods were tried, such as dragging chains along the bottom and fitting cutting devices to boats. In 1862 an 'unusual species of plant or weed' was reported to have appeared in the Circular Line, which rapidly spread to the whole system. This was probably Canadian waterweed which had appeared in the English canals in the 1850s.[7] The introduction of motor boats had lessened the problem in the main channel where the propellers kept a reasonably clear passage but this had tended to reduce efforts directed against the weeds.

The commission summed up the evidence on the Grand Canal:

It appears to be clear from the evidence that the Grand Canal has been allowed to fall into a bad state over a long period of years. . . . We consider it is not expedient that the ownership and maintenance of a public highway should be in private hands. While the Grand Canal Company has useful functions to perform as a carrier, the navigation highway should be transferred to the public authority which we recommend should be set up.

The commission's recommendation that a 'Waterway Board' should be established to administer all the waterways was not implemented and the canal company was left to struggle on.

Traffic continued to decrease and from 1921 to 1926 the dividend on the ordinary shares fell to 2 per cent. The unions, recognising the difficulties of the company, reluctantly allowed some of the war bonuses, which were still being paid, to be reduced. There were constant requests from the unions with respect to holidays, overtime, wages and hours, most of which were turned down by the board. This sometimes led to short strikes and, in August 1923, a strike lasting three months was caused by the bulkers' refusal to handle 'tainted goods'.

In 1929 and 1930 the net revenue improved sufficiently to allow a dividend of 4 per cent on the ordinary shares but this was followed by a sharp decrease in traffic which the board attributed to three causes: the general depression in trade throughout the country, the growing competition from the railways, which had amalgamated in 1924 as the Great Southern Railway and with whom all agreements had terminated in 1920, and lastly the growing competition from road transport. The railway company had adopted a system of free delivery of goods by road from its stations and in order to fight this and other road competitors the board decided in 1931 to purchase two Ford lorries. Prior to 1927 the railway and canal companies had been precluded from operating road services but an Act passed in that year released them from this restriction. Further Acts in 1932 and 1933 limited the operation of road services to railway, canal and shipping companies and to those motor transport companies already in existence.

The rates war with the railway company intensified. A campaign was launched by the GSR of advertising for traffic in exclusively canal territory and the canal company fought back by building up its fleet of lorries to win traffic from the railways. In February 1932 it was minuted 'that correspondence from the GSR be not replied to'. The canal company created the new post of 'canvasser' and the railway company printed cards with 'Send all my goods by Rail', which it distributed to potential customers.

The net revenue of the canal company fell from over £22,000 in 1930 to £14,401 in 1933 and the dividend on the ordinary shares fell to 1 per cent. In June 1933 the board tried to introduce a 10 per cent reduction in wages but this was quickly followed by a week's strike notice from James Larkin of the Workers' Union of Ireland. A stormy meeting followed at which Larkin 'finally objected to all the terms of reference and would not discuss the matter further'. In the end it was settled by arbitration and the company had to agree to retain the existing wage structure.

A serious stoppage occurred in August 1934 over weekend working and the strike dragged on with neither side prepared to accept the award of a court of inquiry. The boatmen grew bitter and they damaged locks and bridges to try to halt byetrader traffic. Some of the men were arrested and, to prevent a deterioration in the situation, a return to work was agreed pending a new inquiry. Work was resumed on 3 December but discussions dragged on and ultimately the company had to concede increases to all employees. The Barrow lock-keepers, who were still only receiving 11s (55p) per week, had asked for an increase of over £1 but they were granted an increase of 4s (20p).

In the 1930s a drainage scheme, carried out by the Board of Works in the upper catchment area of the River Barrow, caused damage to the navigation works. The increase in flow aggravated the difficulties of maintaining the navigation and caused silting in the side canals. Following the hearing of a claim for compensation, the canal company was awarded over £18,000 for 'temporary and permanent damage'. Winches with wire ropes and an 80hp tug were placed on the river to assist the boats upstream but services below Carlow gradually ceased, the company finding it easier to tranship the goods at Carlow and forward them by road.

The war years, with the stringent restrictions on road transport, brought about an increase in trade on the canal, with horse-drawn haulage coming into its own again. The following table illustrates this artificial prosperity:[8]

Year	Co's Boats tons	Bye-traders tons	Total tons
1938	107,441	62,291	169,732
1944	120,649	106,023	226,672
1947	112,002	48,171	160,173

Year	Revenue £	Expenditure £	Net Surplus £	Ordinary Dividend per cent
1938	126,716	112,542	14,174	1
1944	174,365	147,850	26,515	4½
1947	174,712	168,820	5,892	0

The company, finding it difficult to cope with the increase in trade during the war years, passed on the surplus to the bye-traders; they carried out a great deal of the movement of turf to the city in G-boats on loan from the company. It will be noticed that, although the revenue remained the same after the war, the net surplus fell considerably. This was because the war years produced a wages standstill, but when this restriction was removed wage demands of over 50 per cent had to be met. The government allowed an increase of 20 per cent in tolls and freights, which explains why the revenue remained the same when the tonnage fell.

In 1946, encouraged by the increased revenue, the board had decided to build a transhipping shed with electric hoists at Shannon Harbour in addition to purchasing the two large boats for the Shannon trade which had involved enlarging the locks there. This expenditure never really justified itself and the improved facilities were far in excess of requirements when the temporary increase in trade subsided.

Road transport recovered quickly after the war and by 1948 the road services accounted for 27 per cent of the company's income. The tonnage carried by water fell steadily but the increasing revenue, subsidised by the road services, enabled the company to pay an ordinary dividend of 3 per cent in 1948. The canal company was carrying goods by road at canal rates, thus undercutting other road services, and this factor may have influenced the members of a transport inquiry, set up in 1948 under the chairmanship of Sir James Milne, to recommend the amalgamation of the canal company with the proposed new transport authority, Coras Iompair Eireann. The directors resisted this proposal and suggested that the company should give up the carrying trade but continue to maintain the canal as a holding company. They estimated that this would produce a net profit of about £25,000. The merger went ahead, however, and on 1 June 1950 a total of £702,500 in government guaranteed transport stock was issued to the shareholders on a pound for pound basis.[9]

On 17 August 1950 the board met for the last time and one week later, on 25 August, the final meeting of the company was held attended by the board and one shareholder, representing over 500 proprietors. In his address to the company John McCann, the chairman, stressed that the board had not sought the amalgamation, nor had it looked for assistance from the government. Suggestions that the compensation paid to the company's shareholders was excessive were entirely without foundation. An inspection of the company's final balance sheet, he added, would show that the capital of the company was more than represented by tangible assets and that its financial position was extremely sound. He was confident that, although they might have been forced out of the carrying business, 'other and additional interests' would have

earned for the shareholders as good a return on their capital
as that which was now being guaranteed by the government.

John Scott and Charles Calwell saw the company through
the merger but they both retired in 1951. John Dalton, who
had joined the canal company in 1926 and had been assistant
engineer since 1941, was placed in charge of the maintenance of
the Grand and Royal canals and A. J. Knox, the goods agent,
continued to control the carrying trade. When John Dalton
retired from CIE in 1970, one of the last links with the Grand
Canal Company was severed.

After the merger, CIE's accounts for the canals showed an
increasing loss:[10]

		Grand Canal Traffic	
Year	CIE boats	Bye-traders	Total
	tons	tons	tons
1952	89,130	26,561	115,691
1956	89,640	8,775	98,415

		Grand and Royal Canals	
Year	Revenue	Expenditure	Deficit
	£	£	£
1952	149,170	201,902	52,732
1956	163,114	228,236	65,112

The canal company's fleet of lorries had been absorbed in CIE's
fleet and the revenue from this source and from the docks at
Ringsend were not included in these accounts.

Several increases in tolls had been authorised since the 20
per cent rise after the war and the bye-traders were finding it
increasingly difficult to operate economically. In 1957 a committee of inquiry into internal transport was set up under the
chairmanship of J. P. Beddy. This committee heard evidence
that all bye-trader traffic had now ceased and recommended
that CIE should be allowed to withdraw the water transport
service and divert the traffic to the struggling railways; it was
estimated that this would produce an annual saving of £108,000.
The canal boats were withdrawn on 31 December 1959

although some of them remained in service until the following May to facilitate Guinness's Brewery, who had not completed alternative arrangements at Limerick. At the time of the withdrawal the brewery accounted for nearly 40 per cent of the traffic on the canal and the Carlow Sugar Company for another 20 per cent.

A great deal of the traffic found its way on to the roads instead of the railways and the latter did not benefit to the extent that the Beddy committee had anticipated. In retrospect, with the tremendous increase in heavy road traffic, it is a pity that the commercial boats were withdrawn but if they had continued, a heavy expenditure would have been required in modernisation to produce an efficient system and it is doubtful if this expenditure would have been justified. Mr Scott, general manager and director at the time of the merger, considers that canal transport today would be totally uneconomic for any type of commodity, having regard to the restricted size of the canal and the increasing costs of wages and shorter working hours.

The withdrawal of the commercial boats sealed the fate of some of the branches as there was very little pleasure traffic using the canal. The Ballinasloe line, which had carried a good deal of traffic until 1959, was officially closed in 1961 and handed over to Bord na Mona. Today, parts of it have disappeared in bog workings, the section through Kylemore is being used to lay a light railway and at the Ballinasloe end it has been filled in. There had been a small amount of traffic to Odlum's Mill at Portarlington on the Mountmellick Line in the 1950s, but it was officially closed to navigation in 1960 and is now completely derelict. Several low level bridges have been built across it and the section around Portarlington has been filled in as a link road. The Kilbeggan Line, which had not been used since about 1940, was officially closed in 1961 and has been sealed off and drained. An occasional boat had gone through to Naas until 1959 but the section from Naas to Corbally, which had not been used for some years, was closed by a low level bridge just outside Naas in the early 1950s. The Blackwood feeder, which had been used over the years to bring down turf from the surrounding bog, was closed to navigation in 1952 and was subsequently drained and its fate sealed by some low level bridges. The Milltown feeder, which had carried occasional traffic, was closed to navigation about 1945 but is still maintained as the principal feeder to the canal and some pleasure boats have been through to Milltown Bridge in recent years.

The recent development of the River Shannon as a major tourist amenity, which has met with such success, has shown that the Grand Canal system does have a future in this respect. The short branch to Edenderry, which had become impassable with weed, has now been reopened and the possibility of reopening the Naas and Kilbeggan Lines is being investigated. The canalside village of Robertstown has appreciated the potential of the canal and attracts large crowds to its various activities, and Shannon Harbour held its first annual barge rally in 1971, attended by about twelve converted canal boats. Dublin Corporation's plan to take over the Circular Line as a bed for a new sewer with the ultimate objective of laying a motorway along it, was defeated by public pressure and the government has promised that the canal will be retained in any future schemes. Legislation is being prepared to transfer the Grand Canal system, including the Barrow Navigation, from CIE to the Board of Works. The latter already administers the Shannon Navigation and it should then be possible to develop all the waterways under a single authority.

The long history of the Grand Canal Company is at an end but the Grand Canal is just about to enter a new phase.

Notes

NOTES TO CHAPTER 1 (*pages 13–27*)

1. 8 Geo I, c 6 (Ir), 1721; 3 Geo II, c 3 (Ir), 1729.
2. McCutcheon, W. A., *The Canals of the North of Ireland* (1965).
3. 25 Geo II, c 10 (Ir), 1751; Delany, V. T. H. & D. R., *The Canals of the South of Ireland* (1966), pp 18–19.
4. Delany, p 32; (Anon) *Observations on a Pamphlet lately published entitled A Description of the Rival Lines for Inland Navigation etc* (Dublin, 1756).
5. Delany, p 33; (Anon) *Mr Omer's Letter to the Public Controller of Inland Navigation* (Dublin, 1755); (Anon) *Mr Omer's Letter to the Public Controller . . . Examined* (Dublin, 1756); (Anon) *A Description of the Rival Lines . . .* (Dublin 1756).
6. Irish Commons *Journal*, 8 November 1757, VI, p 26; 24 October 1759, VI, app cxcix, No 20; 9 November 1761, VII, app xl; 15 November 1763, VII, app ccxxxvii; Delany, pp 34–6.
7. *Calendar of Ancient Records of Dublin*, vol 11, pp 170 & 265; *ICJ*, 11 November 1763, VII, p 212.
8. *CARD*, vol 11, pp 208, 321, 347, 430; vol 12, p 24; *ICJ*, 22 November 1769, VIII, app cccxxvii; Delany, pp 36–8; Phillips, Henry. 'The Early History of the Grand Canal', *Dublin Historical Record*, vol I (1938).
9. *ICJ*, 22 November 1769, VIII, part 2, app cccxxvii.
10. 11 & 12 Geo III, c 31 (Ir), 1771–2.
11. *CARD*, vol 12, pp 59, 134, 135, 162, 179, 182.
12. O'Brien, Sir Lucius, *Two Letters to the Public* (Dublin 1771); Delany, pp 39–40.
13. *Hibernian Journal*, 14–16 April 1773. The silver trowel used to lay the foundation stone is on loan by CIE to the Civic Museum, 58 South William Street, Dublin.
14. Vallancey, Charles, *Report on the Grand Canal* (Dublin, 1771); Trail, John, *Report on the Grand Canal* (Dublin, 1771); both these reports help to determine the amount of work carried out before 1771.
15. *Letters between Redmond Morres Esq and John Smeaton in 1771 and 1772 etc* (Dublin, 1773).
16. Smiles, Samuel, *Lives of the Engineers* (1874), vol 2 p 303; Rolt, L. T. C., *Great Engineers* (1962).
17. Smeaton, John, *Reports* (1812), vol 2.
18. Delany, Ruth, 'John Trail', *Journal of the County Kildare Archaeological Society*, vol 14, part 5 (1970).

19. Mullins, M. B., 'Presidential Address', 8 November 1859, *Trans Inst Civil Engineers Ireland*, vol 6, p 54.
20. Walker, E. K., 'The Grand Supply', *Canaliana* (Robertstown, Muintir na Tire, 1967).
21. *ICJ*, 26 November 1779, X, p 35; 7 November 1781, X, p 239; 6 November 1783, XI, p 77.

NOTES TO CHAPTER 2 (*pages 47–64*)

1. Mullins, Bernard & M.B., 'Origin and Reclamation of Peat Bog', *Trans ICE Ir*, vol 2 (1846).
2. McCutcheon, p 99; Delany, pp 82–5, 101–2, 158–9.
3. *ICJ*, 16 March 1789, XIII, app clxxi.
4. Smiles, *Lives of the Engineers*, vol 2.
5. Delany, pp 80–3; Delany, Ruth, 'The Royal Canal Shoemaker', *Canaliana* (1971).
6. 29 Geo III, c 33 (Ir), 1789.
7. William Chapman, 1749–1832, 10 *DNB* 57.
8. Weale's *Quarterly Papers in Engineering*, vol 1. This invention is described in detail in a memoir of Chapman.
9. Smeaton, *Reports*, vol 2.
10. *ICJ*, 2 July 1800, XIX, app mlxxxiii.
11. Vallancey and Trail, *Reports on the Grand Canal*.
12. *Journal* of the House of Commons, 1805 (169), IV, 351, pp 15–32; 1812 (366) V, 679, p 153; Delany, p 47.
13. *JHC*, 1805 (169), IV, 351; 1812 (366), V, 679, Report of the Directors-General, p 88.
14. 27 Geo III, c 30 (Ir), 1787.
15. 40 Geo III, c 51 (Ir), 1800.
16. Delany, pp 48–9.

NOTES TO CHAPTER 3 (*pages 65–89*)

1. *JHC*, 1812 (366), V, 679, p 152.
2. Delany, p 50. Chapman, William, *Observations on the Advantages of bringing the Grand Canal round by the Circular Road into the River Liffey* (Dublin, 1785), Father Murphy of Robertstown has the plan showing Brownrigg's direct route from James's Street into the Liffey.
3. *ICJ*, 18 March 1791, XIV, p 392.
4. 31 Geo III, c 42 (Ir), 1791.
5. *Dublin Journal*, 26 April 1796; *Dublin Evening Post*, 23 April 1796; Delany, p 51.
6. Lord Clonmel's Diary quoted in *Dublin Explorations and Reflections by an Englishman* (1917), p 79.
7. De Latocnaye, *A Frenchman's Walk through Ireland*, translated by J. Stevenson (Belfast, 1917).
8. Griffith, Sir John Purser, *The Port of Dublin* (Dublin, 1915).
9. 26 Geo III, c 60 (Ir), 1786; Delany, p 52–3.
10. I am indebted to Professor Skempton for sending me some notes taken from correspondence between Chapman and James Watt and Matthew Boulton

covering his time in Ireland. The correspondence is in the Reference Library and Assay Office, Birmingham. Weale's *Quarterly Papers*, vol 1.

11. *Dublin Evening Post*, 8 March 1788; Meagher, Niall, 'The Naas Branch of the Grand Canal', *Canaliana* (1971); Costello, Con, 'The Corbally Line', *Canaliana* (1967).

12. Rees, D. D., *Cyclopaedia* (1820), under 'oblique arches'; Weale's *Quarterly Papers*, vol 1.

13. Walker, E. K., 'The Grand Supply', *Canaliana* (1969), p 6.

14. *ICJ*, 22 July 1785, XI, p 473; 16 March 1786, XII, p 108, app ccliii; 7 March 1787, XII, p 221; 29 Geo III, c 33 (Ir), 1789; Delany, p 45.

15. *CARD*, vol 12, p 266.

16. *Freeman's Journal*, 2 July 1791.

17. 35 Geo III, c 44 (Ir), 1795; 39 Geo III, c 79 (Ir), 1798; Delany, pp 47, 51.

18. *ICJ*, 23 June 1800, XIX, part 2, app mvi–mxlii; 2 July 1800, app mlxxviii–mlxxxvii; 5 July 1800, app mlxxxix–mxciii.

19. *JHC*, 1805 (169), IV, 351. There are references to this controversy in the records of the directors-general in the Public Record Office, Dublin.

20. *CARD*, vol 15, p 306. The ensuing battle with the GCC is recorded in these records.

21. *Freeman's Journal*, 10 July 1804.

22. *Freeman's Journal*, 14 July 1804, long statement by the GCC and 17 July publication of correspondence. There are further references in the newspapers until agreement in May 1805.

23. Dutton, Hely, *Statistical Survey of County Dublin* (Dublin, 1802), app p 101.

24. *JHC*, 1805 (169), IV, 351, p 26.

25. *JHC*, 1812–13 (61), VI, 317, app 34, pp 74–5, breakdown of tonnage 1809–12 into and out of James's Street, differentiating between Barrow and Shannon Line for inward traffic, and the total traffic handled at Portobello.

26. *JHC*, 1812 (366), V, 679; 1812–13 (198, 266, 284, 283, 79, 91, 61), VI.

27. *JHC* 1812 (366), V, 679, app 16F; 1812–13 (61), VI, 317, app 35, p 76.

28. *JHC*, 1812 (366), V, 679, pp 8, 134; 1812–13 (61), VI, 317, app 35, p 76.

29. *JHC*, 1812 (366), V, 679, app 16B, p 132.

30. 58 Geo III, c 35, 1818; Delany, pp 85–6.

NOTES TO CHAPTER 4 (*pages 90 – 104*)

1. Cloncurry, Lord, *Personal Recollections of the Life and Times of Valentine 2nd Lord Cloncurry 1773–1835* (1850).

2. Smith, Sir William Cusack, *Grand Canal—Defence of the Court of Directors* (Dublin, 1815).

3. Longfield, A. K., 'Prosperous', *J Kildare Arch Soc*, vol 14, No 2 (1966–7). Robert Brooke was a brother of Thomas Digby Brooke, the first trader.

4. I am indebted to the Very Rev A. D. Buchanan, Dean of Kildare, for sending me some extracts from the minutes of the United Parish of Kilmeague and Rathernan.

5. *ICJ*, 2 July 1800, XIX, part 2, app mlxxviii; *JHC*, 1805 (169), IV, 351, app C, pp 78–80; Delany, pp 55–6.

6. *ICJ*, 2 July 1800, XIX, part 2, app mlxxix–mlxxxi; *JHC*, 1805 (169), IV, 351, app B, p 31; Tighe, William, *Statistical Observations Relative to the County of Kilkenny* (Dublin, 1802), app 4–6; Delany, pp 53–5.

7. McCutcheon, pp 106–9.

8. Fulton, Henry, *Three Letters to the Proprietors of Grand Canal Stock* (Dublin, 1838).
9. *JHC*, 1837-8 (145), XXXV, 449, app B 6, tonnage from 1822-37, breakdown of commodities but not divided into traffic into and out of the city.
10. John Macneill (1793?-1880), 35 *DNB* 249.
11. Macneill, John. *Report on the Grand Canal* (Dublin, 1844).

NOTES TO CHAPTER 5 (*pages 105-20*)

1. *Journal* of John Wesley, 22 July 1785, quoted in an article by N. W. English, 'Waterway Travellers in Ireland', *Canaliana* (1967).
2. *Freeman's Journal*, 4-7 February 1786.
3. *Freeman's Journal*, 22-4 December 1792.
4. *Freeman's Journal*, 27-9 December 1792, gives details of the victims; in addition to the family there were 'two amiable young ladies' and 'three apprentices of a cabinet-maker in Aungier Street'. This, with Captain White makes ten; it does not state who the eleventh victim was.
5. DeLatocnaye, *A Frenchman's Walk*.
6. *The Volunteers Journal*, 11 August 1786, quoted in article by N. W. English, 'Eighteenth Century Canal Ephemera', *Canaliana* (1969).
7. I am indebted to Mrs Olive Goodbody, Librarian of the Friends' Library, Eustace Street, Dublin, for allowing me to look through the Leadbeater papers, for which she has produced an excellent index.
8. Phillips, Henry, 'The Passenger Boats', *J Kildare Arch Soc*, vol 10 (1922).
9. Trollope, Anthony, *The Kellys and the O'Kellys*, first published 1848, chapter 8. Lever, Charles, *Jack Hinton: the Guardsman*.
10. Trollope. *The Kellys and the O'Kellys*, chapter 8.
11. Carr, Sir John, *The Stranger in Ireland 1805* (1806).
12. Venedy, Herr J., *Ireland and the Irish during the Repeal Year 1843* (Dublin, 1844), translated by W. B. MacCabe.
13. Rolt, L. T. C., *The Inland Waterways of England* (1950), pp 151-5. Spratt, H. Philip, *The Birth of the Steam Boat* (1958).
14. James Dawson, Patent No 3821, 16 July 1814, 'Producing or communicating motion in or unto bodies wholly or in part surrounded by water or air, by means of the reaction of apparatus on such water or air or upon both of them.' Also Patent No 3996, 14 March 1816.
15. McNeill, D. B., *Irish Passenger Steamship Services*, vol 2 (1971), p 158, also McNeill, *Coastal Steamers and Inland Navigations in the South of Ireland*, Transport Handbook 6, Belfast Transport Museum (1967).
16. James Scott, Patent No 4448, 15 April 1820, 'Combining, adjusting and applying certain mechanic powers and modifications thereof, or an "Accelerating lever-motion" applicable to many purposes.' Also Patent No 4457, 11 May 1820.
    Goldsworthy Gurney, Patent No 5170, 14 May 1825, 'Apparatus for propelling carriages on common roads or on railways.' Also Patent No 5270, 21 October 1825, 'Apparatus for raising and generating steam.'
17. *Proceedings* of the Inst CE, vol 26 (1866-7), discussion which followed a paper by Samuel Healy, quoted in *Canaliana* (1968).
18. *The Saturday Magazine*, No 705, Supplement June 1843, p 247, quotation from a letter to Canal Proprietors by Mr Grahame. I am indebted to Dr Corran, Chairman of IASI, who kindly presented me with this.
19. Ibid.

NOTES TO CHAPTER 6 (*pages 127–44*)

1. I am indebted to Mrs Clare Ferris for making available Robert Whyte's account books. There are detailed articles about them by Eileen Ryan in *Canaliana* (1967–8) and by Ruth Delany in *Canaliana* (1970).
2. Bianconi, M. O'C., and Watson, S. J., *Bianconi* (Dublin, 1962).
3. Ibid, p 114.
4. *JHC* 1812 (366), V, 679, p 121, expenditure (Ir) on the hotels up to 1812:

	Building	Furniture	Total
	£	£	£
Portobello	8,743	2,100	10,843
Robertstown	5,376	2,116	7,492
Tullamore	3,200	1,200	4,400
Shannon Harbour	4,791	267	5,058
		Total	£27,793

There was no separate account kept of Sallins Hotel.
5. See note (1) above.
6. Cooke, John, 'Bog Reclamation and Peat Development in County Kildare', *J Kildare Arch Soc*, Vol 14, No 5 (1970).
7. MacGregor, John. *A New Picture of Dublin* (Dublin, 1821).
8. The accident is reported with an illustration in the *Illustrated London News*, April 1861.
9. I am indebted to N. W. English for drawing my attention to this interesting manuscript in the Nat Lib, Dublin, by F. S. Bourke, 'Gleanings in the West of Ireland' (1836), MS No 10.736.
10. Hayward, Richard, *Where the River Shannon Flows* (Dundalk, 1940), quotes Mr Larkin's letter in full.

NOTES TO CHAPTER 7 (*pages 145–58*)

1. *JHC* 1812 (366), V, 679, p 141.
2. Tighe, *Statistical Observations . . . County Kilkenny.*
3. I am indebted to Dr L. Cullen for drawing my attention to the Hartpole-Bowen and Hartpole-Leckey papers in Trinity College, Dublin (MS No 4813–6, 1933), which provide some information about Doonane colliery before and after the GCC's tenure.
4. James Ryan, Patent No 2822, 12 February 1805, 'Apparatus for boring the earth for coal or other substances.'
5. *JHC* 1812 (366), V, 679, full details of collieries' expenditure, pp 117–20.
6. Sir Richard Griffith, 1784–1878, 23 *DNB* 238, Commissioner of Valuation 1828–68, knighted 1858, author of *Geological and Mining Survey of the Leinster Coal District* (Dublin, 1814).
7. See note (3) above.
8. Chapman, William, *Report on the Navigation of the River Shannon etc* (Limerick, 1791); Delany, p 102.
9. *ICJ*, 18 February, 24 February 1794, XV, pp 310, 318; 23 June 1800, XIX, part 2, app mviii; Delany, pp 104–6.

10. *JHC*, 1805 (169), IV, 351, app C. Details of this controversy in records of the Directors-General in the Public Record Office, Dublin.
11. *JHC*, 1812 (366), V, 679, app 7, pp 307–12; 1812–13 (61), VI, 317, p 19 and app 22–30; Delany, pp 106–8.
12. Delany, p 173 inscription quoted in full also in Rolt, L. T. C., *Green and Silver* (1949), p 226.
13. Williams, C. W., *Observations on the Inland Navigation of Ireland* (1831).
14. *JHC*, 1834 (532), XVII, 141; 1833 (371), XXXIV, 235; Delany, pp 112–20.
15. *JHC*, 1837–8 (142), XXXIV, 203, app A.
16. *JHC*, 1839 (173), XXVIII, 139, p 186.
17. 7 & Vic, c 98, 1844.

NOTES TO CHAPTER 8 (*pages 159–76*)

1. Edwards, R. D., and Williams, T. D., *The Great Famine* (Dublin, 1956), p 123.
2. Thom's *Directory*, 1849–54, contain many statistics including the tonnage carried to and from the city 1842–52, with a breakdown of commodities.
3. Hadfield, Charles, *Atmospheric Railways* (1967).
4. Delany, p 88.
5. I am indebted to Kevin Murray for these details about the formation of the GS & WR and the MGWR.
6. 8 & 9 Vic, c 42, 1845.
7. Lynch, Patrick, and Vaizey, John, *Guinness's Brewery in the Irish Economy* (Cambridge, 1960).
8. Michael Goodbody very kindly lent me some correspondence which he found in the Grand Canal store at Dromineer.
9. Macneill, John, *Report on Screw Steam Boats* (Dublin, 1844).
10. Healy, Samuel, 'Steam Power on the Grand Canal', *Proc ICE*, vol 26, quoted in *Canaliana* (1968).
11. 11 & 12 Vic, c 124, 1848.
12. Griffith, Sir John Purser, *The Port of Dublin* (Dublin, 1915).
13. Thom's *Directory*, 1849–52. The number of boats entering the docks 1844–50.
14. See note (12) above.
15. These negotiations are mentioned briefly in the records of the GS & WR in Heuston Station (Kingsbridge), Dublin.
16. Brief mention in records of MGWR in Heuston Station.
17. Some details of this struggle can be traced in G. R. Mahon's year by year 'Survey of Irish Railways' in *Journal of the Irish Railway Records Society*, commencing vol 3, No 14 (1954).

NOTES TO CHAPTER 9 (*pages 177–94*)

1. Johnston, Henry, 'On the Rathmines Waterworks', *Trans Inst CE Ireland*, vol 9 (1866).
2. Hassard, Richard, 'On the River Vartry as a Source of Supply for Dublin', *Trans Inst CE Ireland*, vol 6 (1861).
3. Inland Waterways Commission 1923, minutes of evidence (unpublished, typescript copy in the Nat Lib, Dublin), 13th day.

4. Ryan, H., 'Reports upon the Irish Peat Industries', part 1 (1907), part 2 (1908), *Econ Proc Royal Dublin Society*, vol 1. Cooke, *J Kildare Arch Soc*, vol 14, No 5 (1970). *Report on Peat of Commission of Inquiry into the Resources and Industries of Ireland* (Dublin, 1921).

5. Hodgson, C., 'Improvements in the Manufacture of Peat Fuel', *Trans Inst CE Ireland*, vol 7, 1862. 'On Manufacture of Compressed Peat Fuel', *Proc Inst Mech E Ireland* (1865).

6. Inland Waterways Commission, evidence of David Sherlock, 11th day (unpublished, see note 3 above).

7. Ibid, evidence of Sir John Purser Griffith, 12th day and James Lindsay, 13th day.

8. D'Arcy, Gerard, *Portrait of the Grand Canal*, Transport Research Associates, 1969, p 88.

9. 1923 Commission, evidence of James Lindsay, 13th day.

10. These figures appear in the minute books and were produced by the board in 1886 in answer to accusations of the shareholders' committee.

11. *Ireland's Gazette*, 24 February 1886.

12. *Irish Times*, 26 February, 8 March 1886. *Freeman's Journal*, 22 February 1886.

13. 57 & 58 Vic, c 26, 1894.

14. A short history of the Barrow Navigation in Delany, pp 126–38. Some of the minute books are in Heuston Station, Dublin.

15. *JHC* (Cd 3717), 1907, XXXIII, evidence of George Tough.

16. *JHC* (Cd 3719), 1907, XXXIII, (Cd 5626) 1911, XIII.

NOTES TO CHAPTER 10 (*pages 195–203*)

1. D'Arcy, Gerard, *Portrait of the Grand Canal* (Transport Research Associates 1969), pp 70–80, gives a very comprehensive list of the different series with all the information available about the individual boats. There is a model of a second series M boat in Robertstown hotel museum.

2. Phillips, Henry, *Dublin Historical Record*, vol 1 (1938); *J Kildare Arch Soc*, vols 9 & 10 (1921–2); *Canals and Inland Waterways Journal*, vol 1 (1919).

3. Quoted in full in *Canaliana* (1971), 'Tough', general manager, 'Allen', cashier.

4. 1910, 1915 and 1920 in 1923 Commission on Inland Waterways, unpublished appendix; 1912 figures in *JHC*, 1918 (130, 136), IV, 465, app 7.

5. *Leinster Leader*, January 1916, quoted in *Canaliana* (1970).

6. The report of the 1923 Commission on Inland Waterways was printed, but the useful appendices and minutes of evidence are available in typescript copies in the Nat Lib, Dublin.

7. *Standard Cyclopedia of Modern Agriculture* (1909), vol 1, p 119, reference by Professor A. N. McAlpine.

8. Tonnage from 1957 *Report of the Committee of Inquiry into Internal Transport*, p 66; other statistics in Grand Canal Company balance sheets.

9. Ibid, para 122

10. Ibid, paras 123, 126.

O

Author's Notes and Acknowledgements

IN writing this history of the Grand Canal Company it has been difficult to avoid repeating information already presented in *The Canals of the South of Ireland*, but in cases where the subject was dealt with in detail in the earlier book, I have given the reference in the notes.

All money transactions of the company appear to have been carried out in Irish currency until January 1826 and to avoid confusion I have pointed this out in each case, but it is not clear whether the company converted to British currency in dealings with the government after the Union in 1800. The conversion rate is £13 Irish to £12 British.

The use of Irish mileage is not so clearly defined. In 1783 the board ordered that milestones be placed along the banks, in English miles from James's Street Harbour on the north bank and in Irish miles from Dublin Castle on the south side. In the same year, when new tolls were introduced, it was specified that the charge was 'per English mile'. However, Irish miles continued to be widely used, for example to denote distances in passenger timetables and in arranging contracts with horse contractors. In the text I have used statute miles and when Irish measurements are intended this is made clear. The conversion rate is 2,240 yards to one Irish mile.

I would like to thank Charles Hadfield, editor of this series, who has been a most helpful adviser. My husband, Douglas, has been very patient throughout and his photographic experience has been very valuable. I am very grateful to Cynthia Rice, who, although heavily committed, drew the harbour plans for me and helped me with the drawing of the maps. I would also like to thank the following people who read the manuscript and offered constructive advice: Dr Louis Cullen, Mr J. Dalton, Dr and Mrs Donaldson, Mr Kevin Murray, Dr Peter Denham and Mr J. Scott. The secretary of Coras Iompair Eireann and his staff were most helpful in enabling me to have access to the records of the company and I would also like to thank the staff of the National Library and Trinity College, Dublin.

I am most grateful to Richard Shackleton for placing at my disposal the unique photographic collection of his grandmother, Mrs Jane Shackleton. These photographs have enabled me to evoke something of the atmosphere of the canal in its most active years, 34(*b*), 51(*a*), 52(*b*), 69(*a*), 70(*b*), 121(*a*), 139(*a*), 140(*a*) & (*b*) and 158(*a*). I would like to thank Dr Corran and the photographic department of A. Guinness & Son who were most helpful in reproducing these photographs and other illustrations for me. Thanks are due to the following for permission to reproduce photographs and line illustrations: the National Museum of Ireland, for the frontispiece; A. Guinness & Son, 70(*a*), 176; Coras Iompair Eireann, 33(*b*) (photographed by Mr D. Bennett); Father P. J. Murphy and Robertstown Muintir na Tire, 34(*a*), figures 8, 9, 11, 12, 14, 17, 20, 21; the National Library of Ireland, 87(*a*); Bord Failte, 87(*b*); Mr J. Dalton, 157(*a*); Deegan-Photo Ltd, 157(*b*); the Misses Molloy, Portumna, 158(*b*); the Kildare Archaeological Society, figure 15; Mr E. Barrett, figure 16; Mr M. Goodbody, figures 22, 24.

APPENDIX 1

Chairmen of the Court of Directors

1772–88*	Chairman elected at each meeting	1813	M. J. Plunkett
1789	Richard Griffith	1814	Lord Cloncurry
1790	Turner Camac	1815	Thomas McKenny
1791	John Macartney	1816	Nicholas Fanning
1792	Colonel Charles Eustace	1817	William Hutton
1793	John Macartney	1818	Beresford Burston
1794	William LaTouche	1819	Robert Harty
1795	Richard Griffith	1820	George Warner
1796	Sir John Macartney	1821	The Hon Rev J. Pomeroy
1797	Joseph Huband	1822	James Dawson
1798	A. C. Macartney	1823	Lord Cloncurry
1799	William LaTouche	1824	Thomas McKenny
1800	Richard Griffith	1825	Nicholas Fanning
1801	Sir John Macartney	1826	Sir J. K. James
1802	A. C. Macartney	1827	Robert Harty
1803	Joseph Huband	1828	The Hon Rev J. Pomeroy
1804–5	Richard Griffith	1829	James Dawson
1806	A. C. Macartney	1830	Lord Cloncurry
1807	Joseph Huband	1831	Sir Thomas McKenny
1808	Benjamin Ball	1832–3	Nicholas Fanning
1809–10	The Hon Rev J. Pomeroy	1834	Sir J. K. James
1811	Lord Cloncurry	1835	James Dawson
1812	Joseph Huband	1836	The Hon Rev J. Pomeroy

* The records are incomplete 1785–9 and there may have been an annual chairman elected before 1789.

1837	Sir Thomas McKenny	1849–82	William LaTouche
1838	Nicholas Fanning	1883–9	Brindley Hone
1839–	The Hon Rev J.	1890	F. deV. Kane
40	Pomeroy	1891	Directors acted in
1841	Nicholas Fanning		rotation until Sept
1842	Sir J. K. James	1891–	
1843	Sir Thomas McKenny	1904	James McCann
1844	Simon Foot	1904	Charles Dillon
1845	Daniel Kinahan	1904–6	Percy B. Bernard
1846	Henry Roe	1906–24	Laurence Waldron
1847	John Barton	1924–50	John McCann
1848	John McDonnell		

APPENDIX 2

Dividends

	per cent		*per cent*		*per cent*
1784	Dividend of £569	1863	$2\frac{3}{8}$	1912	4
	15s (£569.75)	1864–5	$2\frac{1}{2}$	1913	$3\frac{1}{2}$
	pipewater rent	1866	$2\frac{3}{4}$	1914	4
1785–7	none	1867–8	$2\frac{1}{2}$	1915	3
1788	1 for $\frac{1}{2}$ year	1869	$2\frac{3}{4}$	1916	2
1789	1 for $\frac{1}{2}$ year	1870	$3\frac{1}{8}$	1917	$3\frac{1}{8}$
1790	$2\frac{1}{2}$	1871	$2\frac{7}{8}$	1918–20	3
1791	$3\frac{1}{2}$	1872–7	3	1921–6	2
1792	$4\frac{1}{2}$	1878–9	$2\frac{5}{8}$	1927	$2\frac{1}{2}$
1793–7	5	1880	$2\frac{1}{2}$	1928	$3\frac{1}{2}$
1798	$2\frac{1}{2}$ for $\frac{1}{2}$ year	1881	$2\frac{1}{4}$	1929–30	4
1799	none	1882	2	1931	$3\frac{1}{2}$
1800	$2\frac{1}{2}$ for $\frac{1}{2}$ year	1883	$2\frac{1}{8}$	1932	2
1801	5	1884	$1\frac{3}{4}$	1933	1
1802	$5\frac{1}{2}$	1885	$1\frac{11}{16}$	1934	1 for $\frac{1}{2}$ year
1803–9	6	1886	$1\frac{3}{4}$	1935	$1\frac{1}{2}$
1810–11	5	1887–8	$1\frac{13}{16}$	1936	2
1812	$2\frac{1}{2}$ for $\frac{1}{2}$ year	1889	2	1937	$1\frac{1}{2}$
1812–35	none	1890	$1\frac{3}{4}$	1938	1
1836–9	1	1891	2	1939	$1\frac{1}{2}$
1840–7	none	1892	$2\frac{3}{4}$	1940–1	$1\frac{3}{4}$
1848*	1 for $\frac{1}{2}$ year	1893	$3\frac{1}{4}$	1942	$2\frac{1}{2}$
1849	$\frac{1}{2}$ for $\frac{1}{2}$ year	1894–5†	4	1943	$3\frac{1}{4}$
1850	$1\frac{1}{4}$	1896–7	$3\frac{3}{4}$	1944	$4\frac{1}{2}$
1851	$1\frac{1}{2}$	1898–9	4	1945	5
1852	$1\frac{1}{4}$	1900	$3\frac{1}{2}$	1946	$4\frac{1}{2}$
1853	$1\frac{5}{8}$	1901	3	1947	none
1854–9	$2\frac{1}{4}$	1902	$3\frac{3}{4}$	1948	3
1860	$2\frac{1}{8}$	1903–10	4	1949–50‡	none
1861–2	2	1911	$4\frac{1}{4}$		

* In 1848 the stock and loan were consolidated.

† In 1894 the stock was reorganised into preference (3 per cent) and ordinary £10 shares.

‡ In 1950 the shareholders were issued with guaranteed transport stock on a £ for £ basis.

Passage Boats and Steamers

Passage boats*

Name	Date of building	Remarks
Millicent		Sold in 1790. Probably the first passage boat
Duchess of Leinster		In commission in 1790
Macartney		In commission in 1790
Harberton		In commission in 1790. Broken up 1796
Griffith		In commission in 1790. Broken up 1797
Camac		In commission in 1790. 'Unfit for service' 1797
Hudson		In commission in 1790
Huband		In commission in 1792. Broken up 1796
Hatch		In commission in 1792
Eustace	1791	Renamed *Quin* in 1806
Lane		In commission in 1797
Buckingham		In commission in 1797
Hartley		In commission in 1797
LaTouche		In commission in 1797
Thetis		Directors' barge in commission in 1797
Lady Castlereagh	1800	Renamed *Courtney* in 1806
Cornwallis		Renamed *Plunkett* in 1806
Hardwicke		
Lea		Refitted and renamed *Fanning* in 1811.
Gondola		Sold 1803. Brought passengers to 1st lock before Portobello became the passenger terminal
Cash	1805	
Archer	1805	Sold 1834
Scriven	1806	
Griffith	1806	
Huband	1807	
Richmond	1807	
Ball	1807	
Pomeroy	1807	Sold 1834

* This list is made up from references to the boats in the minutes and it may, therefore, be inaccurate because of the custom of renaming boats to honour some particular director or lord lieutenant.

Passage boats cont

Name	Date of building	Remarks
Emily		Sold 1834. Possibly the *Cash* renamed in 1814
Hutton		Sold in 1834. Possibly the *Richmond* or *Ball* renamed
McKenny	1816	Withdrawn as guard boat in 1834.
Lady Caher		Possibly old boat renamed
Hamilton	1819	Sold 1834
Harty	1828	First iron boat built by William Mallet at Portobello. Not a success, sold to Robinson of Athlone in 1843 for conversion to steamer
Lord Cloncurry	1830	Iron boat built by John Marshall
Hibernia	1832	Iron boat built by Courtney Clarke at Ringsend Iron Works, cost £275. Not a success, too heavy. (See p 123)
Hamilton	1833	Built by Edward Murphy of Shannon Harbour
James	1833	Iron boat built by John Marshall, the most successful of the Irish boats. Broken up 1849
Emily	1833	Built by John Marshall?
Fanning	1833	The first of the 'Scotch boats', built by William Houston of Johnstone. Tried out for the first time 1 January 1834.
No 2–No 9 'Scotch boats'	1834–7	Sometimes called by names, *Cloncurry*, *McKenny*, *Dawson* and *Helen*. Broken up or sold as the passage boats were withdrawn.
The Rocket	1834	Experimental steam boat built by Courtney Clarke, not a success.
Corballis	c 1834	Light wooden boat.
Pomeroy	c 1834	Light wooden boat, used between James's Street and 1st lock. Sold in 1849.
?	1838	Wooden night boat, built by John Marshall.
?	1838	Wooden night boat, built by Edward Murphy.
2 steam passage boats	1852	Built by Barrington, Ringsend Dockyard, £230 each, with engines by Inshaw £475 each. Never used as passage boats. Tried out as towing steamers, engines sold in 1861 and hulls used as trade boats.

Steamers

Name	Date of building	Remarks
Shannon	1845	Built by Thomas Wakefield Pim, Hull, for £3,580. Sold in 1869.
Towing steamer No 1	1851	Built by Robinson & Russell, Millwall, for £500, single screw.
Towing steamer No 2	1851	Built by Barrington, Ringsend, for £250. Engines by Inshaw, £200, double screw.

Steamers cont

Name	Date of building	Remarks
Brian Boru *Grand Canal*		Used as towing steamer on Liffey. Sold in 1874. Replaced by a Barrow Navigation Company steamer renamed *Grand Canal* sold 1910
Dublin	1862	Sold in 1910. ⎫ Built by Grendons,
Limerick	1862	⎬ Drogheda
Athlone	1863	Sold in 1917 ⎭
3 towing steamers	1865–6	Built by Grendons, Drogheda. The company eventually had a number of steam tugs *Ivy, Bee, Emu, Ant, Fly, Fox* and *Bat*. Some of them had their engines removed in 1904–5 and were converted into trade boats.
Ballymurtagh		Purchased in 1868 from the Wicklow Mining Company for £650. Sold in 1936.
St Patrick		Purchased 1882 and used for cattle. Sold in 1917.
Lady Annette ⎫ *Linda* *Banba* ⎬ *Louise* ⎭		Barrow Navigation Company steamers. *Louise* sold in 1904 and *Banba* and *Linda* in 1928.
Killaloe	1891	Built by D. M. Cumming, Glasgow for £1,034.
Tullamore	1891	Built by T. B. Seath & Co, Scotland. Sold in 1896.
Portumna	1894	Built by Queenstown and Passage Company. Sold in 1936.
Barrow	1902	Sold in 1917.
Carrick	1902	Sold in 1917.
Motor Boats: *Athy*		Registered motor boat 1912.
Naas	1895	Registered motor boat 1913.
St James	1939	Built by Ringsend Dockyard Company. 73ft by 14ft 8in, bolinder engine. Now used by Irish Floatels.
St Patrick	1935	Formerly *Avon King*. Purchased from Severn Navigation in 1946. 84ft 4in by 15ft 5in. Now used by Irish Floatels.
St Brigid	1931	Formerly *Avon Queen*. Purchased from Severn Navigation in 1946. 85ft 7 in by 15ft 9in. Now owned by O'Brien Kennedy.

APPENDIX 4

Breakdown of Tonnage

Commodities	*1801*[1] *inwards*	*outwards*	*1810*[2] *total*	*1825*[3] *total*	*1844* *inwards*
Grain	1,034	222¾	11,424	23,277	19,807½
Barley	—	—	—	—	—
Potatoes	819¾	—	2,189¾	1,643	2,254½
Sugar beet	—	—	—	—	—
Hay and straw	—	—	414½	266	297¼
Flour	10,338¾	—	15,096½	15,373	26,263
Malt	649¼	15	2,592¾	3,524	2,130¾
Other grain products	550	5¼	1,513¾	2,527	7,364¼
Coal, coke and culm	2,576¾	3,945¼	13,314¼	10,202	3,997¾
Turf and turf briquettes	25,368¾	—	34,097	49,230	28,711½
Peat moss litter	—	—	—	—	—
Bricks	12,677	—	13,930	16,116	45,031½
Other building materials	18,370½	103½	54,929¾	35,740	29,498
Timber	1,431¾	—	4,121¾	770	855¾
Cement	—	—	—	—	—
Manure or dung	—	11,790½	17,912¼	14,361	—
Artificial manures	—	—	—	—	—
Miscellaneous raw products	—	—	—	—	—
Oils and tar	—	—	—	—	—
Iron and machinery	—	—	—	—	—
Porter and ale	—	—	—	—	—
Empties	—	—	—	—	—
Sugar	—	—	—	—	—
Cattle and pigs	—	—	—	96	4,785¾
Salt and herrings	—	—	—	74	—
Other items not listed in that year	8,313¾	12,642½	33,898¾	15,532	12,442¾
Total	82,130¼	28,724¾			183,440¼
Total for that year	110,855		205,435	188,731	total =

[1] Year ending February 1801, *JHC*, 1805 (169), IV, 351, p 26.

[2] Year ending August 1810, *JHC*, 1812–13 (61), VI, 317, app 34, pp 74–5, figures for 1809–12, see chapter 3, footnote (23).

[3] *JHC*, 1837–8 (145), XXXV, 449, app B6, p 52, tonnage for 1822–37 shown.

[4] Thom's *Directories*, 1849–54, tonnage for 1842–52 shown.

1844[4] *outwards*	*1847*[4] *inwards*	*outwards*	1912[5] *total*	*1949*[6] *Co's boats*	*Bye-traders*	*1956*[7] *CIE boats*
—	9,861¼	40,043½	52,921	20,376	14,229	5,376
—	—	—	—	—	212	1,310
—	562½	—	840	1,085	36	—
—	—	—	—	2,266	4,214	4,268
—	767¾	—	1,918	—	—	—
—	16,038¾	—	11,220	4,822	116	1,410
—	2,278	—	23,781	4,673	6,754	10,838
790¾	2,287¼	—	22,121	4,645	265	—
8,918	3,186	14,871¾	37,522	1,041	51	—
—	28,886	—	—	—	—	—
—	—	—	14,800	—	1,147	—
—	20,743¾	—	5,790	208	14	—
906¼	28,467¼	1,329¼	28,484	1,609	—	—
2,004	1,109½	2,408¾	16,850	1,286	113	—
—	—	—	2,447	3,887	—	8,852
17,994½	—	25,494½	3,359	—	—	—
—	—	—	15,759	12,085	931	7,556
—	—	—	1,746	523	—	—
—	—	—	797	892	—	—
2,022	—	1,622¼	2,691	563	8	—
2,158¼	—	7,371	37,568	26,020	1,154	21,259
—	—	—	10,250	7,608	353	3,048
—	—	—	2,184	9,347	—	19,652
—	2,439¼	—	125	—	—	—
2,569½	—	2,614¾	705	449	78	—
18,210½	15,544	36,200¼	14,973	8,077	1,539	6,071
55,573¾	132,171¼	131,956		111,462	31,214	
239,014	264,127¼		308,851	142,676		89,640[8]

[5] *JHC*, 1918 (130, 136), IV, 465, app 7. There is an error of 155 in the total shown and this has been added to other items, leaving the total the same.

[6] D'Arcy, Gerard, *Portrait of the Grand Canal* (Dublin, 1969), p 89.

[7] Year ending March 1956, Report on Internal Transport 1957, pp 66–7.

[8] Bye-traders boats total 8,775, total for the year 98,415.

Summary of System

Line	Terminal Points	Years of Construction	Cost £[1]	Length miles
Main	James's Street Harbour–Lowtown	1756–83	486,599[2]	26
Barrow	Lowtown–Athy	1783–91	Included in above	28½
Shannon	Lowtown-Shannon Harbour	1789–1804	321,841	53
Circular	Ringsend, junction with Liffey–1st lock, Main Line	1790–6	56,959 (with docks 179,108)	3¾ 24½ acres in docks
Naas & Corbally	Main Line near Sallins–Corbally	1786–9 (Naas) 1808–10 (Corbally)	30,768	7¾ (Naas 2½)
Edenderry	Main Line–Edenderry	1797–1802	692	1
Milltown Feeder	Lowtown–Seven Springs Milltown	1780s	included in Main Line	8
Blackwood Feeder	Main Line near Robertstown–Foranfan Reservoir	1780s	included in Main Line	4

[1] Cost in Irish currency until 1826.
[2] This figure, which includes the Barrow Line and feeders (Milltown and Blackwood), includes the cost pre-1772, see * p 78.

Number[3] of Locks	Minimum Size[4] of Locks	Bridges[5]	Aqueducts	Feeders[6]	Comments
18 (including 4 double)	70ft 6 in by 13ft 7½in by 5ft 3¾in	19 (including 1 railway)	Leinster	4	Open to navigation
9 (including 2 double)	70ft 10in by 13ft 6in by 5ft	22 (including 1 railway)	Barrow Grattan Camac	6	Open to navigation
18 (including 1 double)	70ft by 14ft 6in by 4ft 10in	40 (including 4 railway) 1 dismantled	Blundell Huband Charleville Macartney	7	Open to navigation
7	69ft 8in by 14ft 9½in by 5ft 3in	14 (including 1 railway & 1 over docks)	none	none	Open to navigation
5	73ft 6in by 14ft 0½in by 5ft	11 (including 1 railway)	none	3	Closed to Naas 1961; derelict Naas–Corbally
none	—	1	none	none	Open to navigation
none	—	3	none	—	Closed to navigation c 1945
none	—	3	none	—	Closed 1952; derelict, partly filled in

[3] In Ireland the staircase pair is called a double lock and counted as one lock.
[4] Length from mitre to mitre by width by depth on cill.
[5] Minimum headroom 9ft in centre of arch.
[6] Some of the feeders listed have been discontinued.

Line	Terminal Points	Years of Construction	Cost £[1]	Length miles
Ballinasloe	Shannon Harbour–Ballinasloe	1824–8	43,485 (also 2,769 wooden bridge)	14½
Mountmellick	Monasterevan–Mountmellick	1827–31	33,416	11½
Kilbeggan	Main Line Ballycommon–Kilbeggan	1830–5	14,000	8
Barrow Navigation	Athy–St Mullins	1759–1812	239,000	43
Middle Shannon	Portumna–Athlone	GCC's tenure 1801–40	GCC's exp 84,907	36

Number[3] of Locks	Minimum Size[4] of Locks	Bridges[5]	Aqueducts	Feeders[6]	Comments
2	70ft 9in by 14ft 7½in by 5ft	5	none	2	Closed 1961; derelict, partly filled in
3	70ft 4in by 14ft 1in by 5ft 3in	17[7] (including 2 railway)	Triogue	2	Closed 1960; derelict, partly filled in
none	—	10	Silver River	none	Closed to navigation 1961
23 (including 1 double)	80ft 2in by 13ft 8in by 4ft	16 (including 1 railway)	—	—	Open to navigation
4[8]	80ft by 16ft by 6 ft[8]	6[8] (including 3 over Meelick canal and Shannon Harbour wooden bridge	—	—	Navigation, altered in 1840s, open today

[7] Three of these no longer exist as one section is now a road.
[8] These figures related to the GCC's tenure.

APPENDIX 6

The Establishment

In 1810[1]

Secretary and his clerk.
Supervisor of Works (subsequently promoted engineer).
Paymaster (and Land Agent).
Book-keeper and his clerk.
Broker, Storekeeper, Treasurer's Clerk, Comptroller, Accountant.
Wharfinger (and Parcel Clerk) at Portobello.
Collectors at:

James's Street	Monasterevan	Tullamore
Portobello	Athy	Gillen (and Cornalour)
Hazelhatch	Naas	Shannon Harbour
Lowtown	Edenderry	Portumna
Milltown	Philipstown (Daingean)	

Overseers: (1) Shannon Line and River Shannon.
          (2) Old Line Dublin to Athy.
          (3) Kildare Canal (Naas and Corbally Line).
3 men in care of supplies.
1 man in care of rope for River Barrow crossing.
1 man to check on Barrow trade.
1 man to distribute oil to lock-keepers.
1 man in charge of boats in Huband Harbour.
51 lock-keepers, 4 River Shannon lock-keepers, 1 Kildare Canal
    lock-keeper.
6 Turnpike gatekeepers.
Ringsend Dockmaster and 5 assistants.
Watchman and porter at James's Street.
2 Messengers.
Passage boat Inspector and 7 assistants at country stations.
6 Masters and 2 supernumeraries.

[1] JHC 1812 (366), V, 679 p 244-9.

7 Steerers.
7 Stopmen.
11 Bellringers.
8 Horse Contractors.
3 Hotelkeepers.
Colliery Manager, 6 clerks, 4 overseers, 4 enginemen, 6 smiths,
    5 carpenters, 20 watchmen, a storekeeper, a surgeon attending
    the colliers.

An estimate of the establishment about 1910[2]

General manager.
Chief clerk and 2 assistants.
Secretary and assistant.
Chief accountant and 6 clerks.
Cashier and 3 clerks.
Engineer, assistant engineer and a clerk.
Goods agent and 7 clerks.
Storekeeper and clerk.
Caretaker (and messenger).
Horsing establishment:
    (this establishment was   horsing superintendent,
    gradually decreased after   stableman, farrier, harnessmaker,
    the introduction of the   several labourers,
    motor boats in 1911)   drivers (who led the horses).
5 carpenters

4 fitters (number increased after 1911).
2 blacksmiths.
6 shipwrights.
1 painter.
1 covermaker.
10 labourers.
Staff of fitting shop at Shannon Harbour.
10 regular 'bulkers' who loaded and unloaded the boats (additional
    bulkers were employed when necessary).
8 checkers who sorted and checked the goods.
Several horse dray drivers (later lorry drivers).
Agents at 38 stations, who employed local labour as required to
    load and unload boats and to deliver goods.
75 lock-keepers.

[2] I am indebted to Mr J. Dalton for his estimate of the company's
    establishment.

P

3 men per boat (increased to 4 with the motor boats but no horse driver required); an average of 60 to 70 boats were engaged in the company's carrying trade.

About 15 men on Shannon steamers and towing steamers.

About 15 men on maintenance boats.

A number of bankrangers.

Ringsend dockmaster and 4 assistants.

Grand Canal Company Records

In order to reduce the number of notes, reference has not been given to the information drawn from the Grand Canal Company's records. These records are in the custody of Coras Iompair Eireann at Heuston Station (Kingsbridge). The following is a list of some of the records:

The minute books of the court of directors 1772–1950, volumes 1–121. Volumes 5, 6, 10, 12, 17, 19 and 27 are missing. These volumes are well indexed.
Half yearly reports of the directors, 1807–1950.
Half yearly accounts, 1886–1950.
Some chairman's agenda books.
Some committee books, 1802–7.
Some carrying trade committee books, 1879–86.
Accounts of work on the middle Shannon, 1802–8.
Some letter books, 1886–1950.
Legal documents, titles, etc.
Information about stock and loanholders.

Index

References to illustrations are printed in italics